"David Power and Michael Downey offe[r] the triune God to a world anguished by [..] degradation, and the loss of a sense of purpose and direction. Their praxis theology of the life-giving Word and love of God made tangible in the particularities of cosmic and human history speaks to the crises and suffering of our time. They invite us to a Eucharistic table in which wounded and broken bodies are remembered and restored to communion in the heart of the divine life that impels us to live justly in the world."

—Elizabeth Groppe
Associate Professor of Theology
Xavier University

"As a teacher of theology at the undergraduate level, I appreciate clear treatments of Christian doctrine. David Power and Michael Downey have written such a work on the Trinity. They have not only traced the history of diverse treatments of the Trinity but have incorporated contemporary intercultural and intercontinental insights in their interpretation of this central Christian doctrine. Those who profess faith in the Triune God and strive to live a just life in a multicultural context will heartily welcome this fantastic contribution to the ongoing conversation on the Trinity."

—Linh Hoang, OFM
Assistant Professor of Religious Studies
Siena College

Living the Justice
of the Triune God

David N. Power, OMI

Michael Downey

A Michael Glazier Book

LITURGICAL PRESS
Collegeville, Minnesota

www.litpress.org

We would like to acknowledge the work of Hans Christoffersen, publisher, and Lauren L. Murphy, managing editor.

—MD and DNP

A Michael Glazier Book published by Liturgical Press

Cover design by David Manahan, OSB. Illustration by Frank Kacmarcik, OblSB. Photo courtesy of Thinkstock/Stockbyte.

Excerpts from documents of the Second Vatican Council are from *Vatican Council II: The Basic Sixteen Documents*, by Austin Flannery, OP © 1996 (Costello Publishing Company, Inc.). Used with permission.

Scripture texts in this work are taken from the *New Revised Standard Version Bible* © 1989, Division of Christian Education of the National Council of the Churches of Christ in the United States of America. Used by permission. All rights reserved.

1   2   3   4   5   6   7   8   9

Library of Congress Cataloging-in-Publication Data

Power, David Noel.
   Living the justice of the Triune God / David N. Power, Michael Downey.
      p. cm.
   "A Michael Glazier book."
   Includes index.
   ISBN 978-0-8146-8045-2 — ISBN 978-0-8146-8046-9 (e-book)
   1. Social justice—Religious aspects—Catholic Church.   2. Trinity.
   3. Catholic Church—Doctrines.   I. Downey, Michael.   II. Title.

BX1795.S62P69   2012
261.8—dc23   2011042543

Contents

Introduction

In 2003 David Power published an article titled "On What Founda-tions? The Christian Witness to the Justice of the Divine Trinity."[1] In this he evoked the plea of John Paul II for a new foundation on which humanity could build a future in the face of the collapse of order, justice, and peace, as well as the pope's statement in *Fides et Ratio* (93) that the major task of theology today is to probe the mystery of the divine *kenosis* in the economy of salvation. A year later Power could have cited the af-firmation in *Ecclesia de Eucharistia* (20) that the eschatological character of Christian memorial necessarily entails a commitment to the service of justice in this world. In that same article, he went on to examine how some developments in the theology of the Trinity have linked this mys-tery with the church's mission to pursue the cause of justice, peace, and reconciliation in the service of the human community. It was then Mi-chael Downey's inspiration that, by working together, the concerns of the article could be developed into a book-length manuscript. The present volume is the fruit of theological conversations and of individual and joint research and writing efforts that span the course of several years.

In recent decades mission statements from churches and church federations have included a commitment to the cause of the poor, to the pursuit of peace and justice, and, even more recently, to the protection of creation as a condition for the future of humanity and cosmos.[2] Typical of such statements is the 1982 affirmation of the Central Committee of the World Council of Churches:

---

[1] David N. Power, "On What Foundations? The Christian Witness to the Justice of the Divine Trinity," *Theoforum* 34 (2003): 155–79.

[2] For examples see *New Directions in Mission and Evangelization: Basic Statements*, ed. James A. Scherer and Stephen B. Bevans (Maryknoll, NY: Orbis Books, 1992).

Whether among the secularized masses of industrial societies, the emerging new ideologies around which societies are organized, the resurging religions which people embrace, the movements of workers and political refugees, the people's search for liberation and justice, the uncertain pilgrimage of the younger generation into a future both full of promise and overshadowed by nuclear confrontations—the Church is called to be present and to articulate the meaning of God's love in Jesus Christ for every person and every situation.[3]

For the Catholic Church, it was *Gaudium et Spes*, The Pastoral Constitution on the Church in the Modern World, promulgated by the Second Vatican Council, that charted a fresh map for the church's self-understanding vis-à-vis the wider human enterprise. After affirming the centrality of the paschal mystery, *GS* 22 goes on to declare: "this holds true not only for Christians but also for all people of good will in whose hearts grace is active invisibly. For since Christ died for everyone, and since all are in fact called to one and the same destiny, which is divine, we must hold that the holy Spirit offers to all the possibility of being made partners, in a way known to God, in the paschal mystery."

This legacy is even better understood when *GS*, most notably paragraph 22, is read together with the closing messages of the council given on December 8, 1965. Though sometimes criticized because they were not submitted to conciliar scrutiny and vote, these messages read at the closing of the council by Pope Paul VI and several cardinals could be said to highlight how its genuine concerns were to be transmitted to various groups of people: world leaders; people of thought and science; artists; women; the poor, sick, and suffering; workers; and youth. This could be seen as the final testament of the council: turning its energy outward in an embrace of all that is worthy and noble in the gift and task of the *humanum*, a clear recognition and affirmation of the common vocation of all humanity.

In a similar vein John Paul II's encyclical *Redemptoris Missio* adopted the conciliar accent on the church's service of the reign of God in the world. Its mission to proclaim Christ includes the mission of transforming the world in and through love, a transformation already begun by the Christ of God. "The kingdom of God is meant for all [hu]mankind, and all people are called to become members of it" (*RM* 14). The action

---

[3] Ibid., 55.

of God through Word and Spirit is found beyond the confines of Christian believers and constitutes a foundation for dialogue and engagement with all who seek the common good of humanity. Such a vision of the reign of God entails "fostering dialogue between peoples, cultures and religions, so that through a mutual enrichment they might help the world to be renewed and to journey ever closer to the kingdom" (*RM* 17). When Pope John Paul II asks on what foundations humanity's welfare may be built, he rightly points to these as common interests among those who appeal to human ingenuity and those who look to God in faith.

Since the emergence of the ecumenical movement, and since the event of the Catholic Church's Second Vatican Council, it has become commonplace to say that in the work of evangelization it is necessary to "read the signs of the times" and to work shoulder to shoulder with others who seek to promote the fullness of human flourishing. For this to be possible the church in its members has to be present in those places where the future of humanity is being worked out. John Paul employs the image of the *Areopagus* (borrowed from Acts 17:22) as a symbol of the new locales in which the Good News must be proclaimed and to which the mission of Christ is to be directed (*RM* 37). Of these various locales, the new *areopagi*, John Paul singles out the fields of communications, culture, scientific research, and international relations that promote dialogue and open up new possibilities for a common interest in promoting justice and peace. Solutions to pressing problems are to be studied, discussed, and worked out precisely in these and other *areopagi*, problems and concerns such as urbanization; the lot of the poor; the aspirations of the young; the migration of peoples of other faiths to traditionally Christian countries; peace and justice; the development and the liberation of peoples; the rights of individuals and peoples, especially those of minorities; the advancement of women and children; plans for safeguarding the created world (*RM* 37). John Paul also takes stock of the desperate search for meaning, the need for an inner life, and a desire to learn new forms and methods of meditation and prayer (*RM* 37). The mission is to take up these and the other pressing concerns, bringing the Gospel of Christ to bear on all of them. In so doing, the Christian community is at the service of "furthering human freedom by proclaiming Jesus Christ" (*RM* 39).

With the passing of the years, the connections between justice, peace, and ecological equilibrium have become more apparent. This is now part of Christian teaching, whether of the World Council of Churches, the green Patriarch Bartholomew of Constantinople, or of Popes John Paul and Benedict XVI. In his message for World Peace Day 2010, Benedict made the connection quite apparent in the aphorism, "If you want to cultivate peace, preserve the creation." While this calls for concrete efforts on the part of societies, both local and global, he made it clear that, in light of revelation, Christians must seek out humanity's true place in the whole order of God's creation. This is found, of course, beginning with the book of Genesis but comes even more to light in what is said in the New Testament about the role of Christ and of the Spirit in creation.

The Second Vatican Council and the later exercise of the magisterium looked at the signs of the times in the sense given the expression by Pope John XXIII. He encouraged Christians to discern what is going on in the world by looking at those indicators, positive and negative, which offer insight into the life of persons, peoples, and communities in the contemporary world. To relate this to the eschatological memorial of Christian worship, the meaning of the signs of the times has to be complemented by the eschatological sense of the signs found in the Scriptures (cf. Matt 12:38-40). These have to do with the manner of God's action in the world, which is not foreseeable in the pattern of the human unfolding of events. Rather, they have to do with what it means to await or expect God's appearance and intervention in ways that often interrupt and disorient, providing a new sense of hope and possibility. Foremost is the "sign of Jonah," the sign of victory over sin and death through the self-gift of Jesus Christ.

At the time of the Second Vatican Council, it was a group of bishops calling itself The Church of the Poor that was most attentive to the biblical sense of signs, locating them especially in the world of the poor and in all that promised them true liberation or freedom. As Popes John Paul II and Benedict XVI have pointed out, the promise and hope of eternal life in a final conquest of the powers of death is essential to hope. At the same time, reading the signs includes a hope for authentic improvement of human life on this earth in all its dimensions. Commitment to this kind of justice has to mean that the church not only aids the poor. It has an obligation in mission and in conscience to listen to them as specially chosen interpreters of the kingdom of God that is promised in the covenant with the Jewish people and in the Gospel.

In this work we want to articulate an order of justice that is shaped by the action of the Trinity as its presence emerges in the work of creation and redemption. This could be called a praxis theology since it does not start with a theory and then move on to practice. At times the word "praxis" is used as though synonymous with "practice." As used here, "praxis" means considering what inspiration can be discerned inherent to a set of human actions directed to an end. It is the unveiling of activities' reasons, motivations, and finalities. This is not raw action but the kind of doing whose meaning is expressed through verbal and symbolic language. To take a praxis approach to the theology of the Trinity is to ask how the inspirations of Word and Spirit as communion in divine life meted out to the world in different times and places are discovered in the blending of activity, expressions of purpose, faith, and hope. Praxis is thus understood as the effort to understand how practice is grounded in the orientations of the human spirit and in the beliefs and ideals to which appeal is made when God's name is invoked.

In attending to biblical stories and the signs of the times in our present era, we look for the movements of Word and Spirit, sent by the Father, in the operations of the world and of human persons and communities. To discern a trinitarian praxis is then to see how the quest for justice, peace, reconciliation, and harmony with creation is guided by consent to the inspirations of Word and Spirit, sent by the Father into the world. In this triune self-communication, God, by Word and Spirit, participates in the human drama of the pursuit of the good even as it is assailed by sin. The contest with the powers of Satan, illustrated in the story of the trial of Jesus in the wilderness where he was driven by the Spirit at the outset of his mission, is always part of the story of the world's peoples.

The pursuit of justice is central to the Christian life and constitutes a distinctive "spiritual life." What is needed is a Christian spirituality that grounds the quest for justice on the part of those who seek to live by the gift of the Spirit in their own time and place, in a world that is crying out for divine justice, for God's own justice. The *Catechism of the Catholic Church* (CCC) itself provides some clues in the quest for constructing an integrated and integrating approach to the whole of the Christian life in the Spirit, inclusive of an ethic of social justice springing from the Divine Trinity. As is known to its readers, the *CCC* is comprised of four parts, or, said differently, the *CCC* is constructed in a way that it rests on four pillars: (1) belief, (2) worship, (3) morality, and (4) prayer. An integrated and integrating approach is alert to all four as these constitute the household of Christian faith and practice. Our attempt here is to start with the call to moral action and to find how the other areas of Christian life relate to this and this to them. In its treatment of social justice (CCC 2419–49) in the section on the moral life, the *Catechism* is sparse enough. It is completed by the *Compendium of the Social Doctrine of the Church*[4] published some years later. Within the praxis approach adopted, our aim is to point to how this central mystery illuminates all the other mysteries of the Christian faith (CCC 234). Grasping the demand for a just life from within contemplation of the Trinity, we can see what inspires prayer and how a sacramental life that is ordered by its trinitarian orientation must include the desire for justice. With liturgy being the source and summit of our participation in the Divine Communion, indeed a share in God's own justice, the moral and spiritual life are moored in both memory and in hope. What emerges in the way of an ethic does not take the form of prescription and command but is found, rather, in the pool of a community's discernment and in anticipation of the fulfilment of the divine promise.

This work is distinctive in at least three ways. First, while the option taken for a trinitarian theology using the analogy of Word and Love much indebted to Augustine, Aquinas, and Karl Rahner is not unique, what is distinctive is the explicit attention given to the communal, inter-subjective, cultural, and linguistic embodiment of the workings of Word and Spirit sent by the Father. "Word is Love heard and seen." Word is the love of God visible, tangible, and audible. "Spirit is the principle of Love's creativity and bonding," the indwelling, invisible dynamism of God's love creating, animating, bonding, and uniting. "In the Word and the Spirit, God is speaking and breathing. Word is what is said, Spirit is the saying. What is said in the saying is Love."[5]

Second, pursuing justice revolves around openness to the work of the Word and Spirit in this world. What is distinctive of the approach in this volume is the emphasis given not simply to acting justly but to living with, in, and from the justice of the triune God by which we are justified.

Third, and finally, explicit attention is given to the sacramental and liturgical grounding of a Christian understanding of both justice and the triune God.

The work is developed in five chapters. In the first chapter, attention to the importance of a praxis-grounded understanding of justice in light of divine presence and gift is offered as key to the understanding

---

[4] The Pontifical Council for Justice and Peace, *Compendium of the Social Doctrine of the Church* (Washington, DC: USCCB Publishing, 2005).

[5] Michael Downey, *Altogether Gift: A Trinitarian Spirituality* (Maryknoll, NY: Orbis Books, 2000), 86.

sought in the book. The other dimensions of Christian life—namely, belief, prayer, and sacrament—are seen in their relation to ethical commitment pursued in God's name. Chapter 2 provides an overview of how the theology of the revelation of God as Father, Son/Word, and Spirit has developed in contemporary writers in the face of suffering and injustice. While several theological orientations and systems are taken into account, an option is taken for a trinitarian theology that is grounded in the mission and work of Word and Spirit in human action and in the cosmos. This is done in preference to considering the life of the Trinity in itself as a model for human social being and action. The third chapter explores the names and the naming of God in light of the specific, or particular, experience of a people or peoples, a name and naming that must always speak of and speak to the experience of human suffering. The order or ordering of divine justice emerges from these various names and ways of naming, and this is the focus of the fourth chapter. Fifth, when the church is concerned with the action of divine justice, those who bear the name of Christ find their moorings and a sense of cohesion when they gather in memory and hope at the Eucharist. This final chapter, then, looks to the Eucharist as source and summit, origin and end of all human striving, at the heart of which is the cry for justice and the emergence of hope.

CHAPTER 1

Call for a Praxis Theology of Divine Justice

The conciliar document *Gaudium et Spes* opened up a way of doing theology which relates the Gospel directly to contemporary historical and cultural realities. Instead of simply enunciating doctrines from which to draw conclusions about what is happening in the world, it took currents of thought and expression as conversation partners. Looking at what is presented as the signs of the times, *GS* asked how these might be interpreted in the light of the Gospel. The assumption was that while there is much evil and suffering in the world, God is at work through the Word and the Spirit in all that is happening: in economic and social developments; in philosophies and world religions; in cultural traditions and their current manifestations; and in all manner of communication, local and global. The way of situating the church in the world was carried forward by Paul VI in the encyclical *Populorum Progressio*, wherein the pope was more specifically attentive to worldwide poverty and discrimination and to the efforts, both religious and secular, to secure for all peoples an "authentic human development." This he located not merely in economic progress but in allowing peoples to bring to completion their particular personal, social, and cultural capabilities.

In the latest in a series of social encyclicals, Benedict XVI's *Caritas in Veritate*, a new world order is envisioned wherein, amid forces of globalization of the human community, justice is motivated and given form through charity. The encyclical is intended to carry forth the message of the church's social encyclicals, especially Paul VI's *Populorum Progressio*, in light of developments in our own day. Charity in truth, or "truth-filled love" (*CV* 79), is the principle not only of "micro-relationships" (friends, family, communities) but of "macro-relationships" (social, economic, political). This truth-filled love in the public sphere is what will

1

bring about a sustainable economy that is just and flourishes in charity. Economic structures that put profits before persons fail on both counts: justice and charity.

Benedict articulates a vision of a renewed social order in which the human person as God's creation, and the place given humanity in the order of things, is central. He writes: "the primary capital to be safeguarded and valued is man [*sic* in the English translation though *homo*, not *vir*, in Latin], the human person in his or her integrity" (25). Further, "in development programmes, the principle of the centrality of the human person, as the subject primarily responsible for development, must be preserved" (47). Citing *Gaudium et Spes* Benedict maintains: "Man [*sic*] is the source, the focus and the aim of all economic and social life" (*GS* 63). His understanding of such a renewed social order in which the human person is the source, focus, and aim of economic and social life rests on a foundation which is charity itself, that is, the God whose name above all names is love. A new world order is woven by living according to the life of the divine Trinity: "Charity is love received and given. It is 'grace' (*cháris*). Its source is the wellspring of the Father's love for the Son, in the Holy Spirit. Love comes down to us in the Son. It is creative love, through which we have our being; it is redemptive love, through which we are recreated" (*CV* 5).

What is worthy of note is that with the vision offered in this encyclical, the church has given moral authority to efforts to work out a solution to the massive problems we are facing, particularly as these affect the poor of the earth, who are to be considered not a burden but a resource. Its message is built on the theological foundations that are grounded in the economy of the Three-in-One Love, the communion of Father, Son, and Spirit. As the encyclical states, this does not foster sentimental and degenerative forms of love. It is a love that is one with the search for truth: "Through this close link with truth, charity can be recognized as an authentic expression of humanity and as an element of fundamental importance in human relations, including those of a public nature" (*CV* 3).

Given currents of globalization and massive economic breakdown on the world scene, together with the emergence of strong waves of religious fundamentalism, the practice of religion which is guided by life-giving energies and which is communicated through symbolic expression can offer hope for peoples and communities striving for human flourishing within their own particular life situations, each searching for a sense of origin and destiny in its own way. A sense of the presence of the God of justice, of justice poured out in self-communication, offers an inspiring vision by which to mobilize peoples and local communities to live in the world in such a way as to swim against the tide of those negative currents of globalization which risk obliterating a true sense of communion at the local level, thereby eliminating any real possibility of true communion on the larger world scene.

In pursuing this end, dialogue with secular thought is both possible and necessary and is built on the recognition of the legitimate interests in the person, social order, and justice which rational thought has brought to the fore. John Paul II and Benedict XVI have both considered conversation between faith and secularism important. Secularism is thought of as a way of conceiving and promoting the common good without resort to faith. If dialogue is possible it is because of reason's openness to the transcendent, however this is formulated. On the way to his 2010 visit to Portugal, Benedict affirmed that "the presence of secularism is something normal" but that there is no inherent opposition between "secularism and a culture of faith."[1] Reason and faith can dialogue with benefit for the common good of world order.

If we are to offer a praxis theology of Trinity we need to present some grasp of our current human and cultural condition. Hence, in this chapter we will look at some insights into contemporary life and then offer some reflections on what it means to read the signs of the times in the light of the Gospel, finding therein the movements of Word and Spirit, the communion offered in the divine mystery which continues to be revealed in God's actions in the universe. The insights into the present are based especially on the contributions to thought of the theologian David Tracy and of the philosopher Jürgen Habermas. The reason for choosing Tracy is that he has taken many currents of thought from around the world into account, whereas Habermas is considered for his way of interrelating the particular and the global in the desire to see how a just human development might come about.

Naming the Present

To go further with a praxis consideration of the mystery of the Trinity and its demand for justice, we have to situate ourselves in the world

---

[1] Benedict XVI, "Portugal Visit: Remarks Aboard Plane," *Origins* 40, no. 3 (May 27, 2010): 34.

and in the church of our time in order to have insight into what happens among us. In our global reality many currents are at work in weaving local and global patterns. Much of what people suffer within the larger evolution of global economics and social patterns can be attributed to the more perverse consequences of the secularization of thought and affect. Nevertheless, to focus solely on this can offer too ready a dismissal of some currents. A better analysis is needed. In a 1990 article taking stock of developments since the Second Vatican Council, David Tracy named those currents of thought which Western theology usually seeks to take into account.[2] Borrowing considerably from his presentation, the following factors in the development of thought may be noted.

Key to the understanding of Modernity is its attentiveness to all that is historical rather than permanent. So much in human living, social and personal, so many of the values held dear, so much cultural and artistic representation, is dependent on historically fluctuating realities that it is well nigh impossible to speak of a necessary continuity in human affairs. What makes up the cultural and social milieu is marked by contingent events, by personalities, by passing ambitions, by efforts to dominate and subjugate, by geographical and climactic conditions, so that an appeal to legal, natural, or religious absolutes is called into question. Among many, then, the effort to establish rational norms and procedures seemed necessary and fundamental. In other words, they looked for sets of rational principles to safeguard the rights of persons and determine the norms of social behaviour. This was accompanied by confidence in the probing and findings of science to unlock nature's secrets and humanity's inventive abilities, allowing human enterprise to build a better future.

Challenged by advertence to historicity, writers such as Wilhelm Dilthey and Friedrich Schleiermacher asked how communities and readers centuries later could have the same faith as those who knew Jesus, who followed him in his comings and goings, who ate and drank with him, or who wrote down the gospel story in the first place. The Catholic Church found it hard to deal with these issues, both the need to be open to rational inquiry and the need to reckon with its own historical conditioning. Hence it retreated into what is called its antimodernistic phase, becoming dependent on the voice of magisterial authority and

---

[2] David Tracy, "On Naming the Present," *Concilium* no. 1 (1990): 66–85.

on claims to the knowledge of the natural law inscribed in the universe and in the essential constitution of the human person.

Only quite recently has the church to greater or lesser degrees taken up these basic and legitimate issues raised by Modernity. Without relying on a stubborn and immovable metaphysical construct, Christians may keep alive the quest for a transcendental origin and destiny to humanity, and indeed to creation, which enables believers to avoid total relativity in face of change. This entails the effort to grasp, in theory and in practice, how a community may live from what is made manifest in historical event, even while it admits the historicity, or the fluidity, in the ways in which knowledge of the event and of its implications is transmitted. The Scriptures, lived Christian spirituality, spiritual and doctrinal writings, are always less than the event and yet a testimony to the event or events in which hearers of the Word confess God to be present and active in the human story and in creation. In other words, Christians perforce live within historically conditioned and changing circumstances which affect their own forms of being as community in the world. Yet they always turn to the retrieval in the midst of change of the events which they confess as God-events. This gives narrative a foundational character in confessing the faith since event is not retrievable as a series of facts but only as it is narrated. This principle of the narrativity of human existence and of revelation restores a mode of conversation with Modernity and with all "others" since even the most rational are invited to recognize how much personal, communal, and social identity depend on narrative and narrative tradition.

Coming out of an antimodernist period, whose sentiments were embodied in the antimodernist oath imposed on candidates for ordination and on teachers of theology, the Catholic Church had to come to terms with the gains of the Enlightenment and of Modernity. This meant working with concerns for human rights in society and church, extending the right of human development and participation in the common good to all members of society and to all peoples, as this is expressed in the United Nations 1947 Charter of Human Rights. It meant integrating philosophical perspectives on the human person coming from writers such as Max Scheler and Gabriel Marcel, as John Paul II indicated in his encyclical *Fides et Ratio* (1998), and valuing the intersubjective in human and social growth, as has been done by Jürgen Habermas in his robust retrieval of Enlightenment gains put to the quest for a more just social order.

Looked at from another angle we can see how swings to individualism and privatization, categorized even as hedonism, elicited a neoconservative and postliberal reaction on the part of many Christian writers. This has meant a studied return to the Word and to the gospel story, together with an effort to retrieve the mystery, not only the teaching, of Christ as core to the move toward a new social order. For some this entailed a refusal to think that Modernity adds anything to an understanding of the Gospel. For some Catholics in particular this reaction has meant the effort to retrieve a strong central government and some of the liturgical practices of the pre–Vatican II era, deemed to be representative of the truly holy.

A broad disillusionment with religion, with reason, with human traditions, with authority, with all that falls under the rubric of culture, is well known in today's world. This is sometimes described as the postmodern condition. Some see this as purely negative and use the term postmodernism in a pejorative sense, seeing it as a way of living in a world that is said to have no viable future and no objective truth on which to build. As with secularism, however, it is possible to rush to too hasty a dismissal of the postmodern and so miss the positive contributions of those who see the limits of the modern as well as of the traditional. Even what is thought to be the needed deconstruction of models of belief, of action, of social unity, and of the natural world because of their ideological hold, opens up fields of creativity that have been long held in check.

At the risk of oversimplification, we point to three hallmarks of a postmodern sensibility. First, since views of reality are not given but constructed, there is suspicion of universal and normative claims, of the prevailing order of things. This is especially because of the reality of historical evil which breaks in and unsettles our sense of order and of divine providence. The interruptive character of history, the suffering and horror perpetrated by powerful elites and ideological victors, calls into question any claim to have a complete hold on truth. Second, there is a suspicion of Modernity's efforts to compartmentalization and specialization. This is true not only of institutions but also of the human person who, in postmodern worldview, is not a self-constructed, self-subsistent self. Nor is the human person a composite of various components or faculties, the premier of which is reason, or rationality, narrowly understood. The human being desires integration in relation to others in community and within a tradition. Third, there is the affirmation that particularity, specificity, and diversity are not at odds with unity and wholeness. Whereas Modernity has made of particularity and unity rivals and competitors, a postmodern worldview sees them as dialectically inseparable.

The implications of a postmodern sensibility for Christian living are wide-ranging. Here our remarks will be limited to two. First, with its recognition of the limits of the project of constructing a self-subsistent autonomous self, there is room for greater attention to other dimensions of the self in understandings of human personhood, especially relationality, community, and the need for tradition in human flourishing. Second, postmodernity's awareness of interruption, discontinuity, and disorientation is not inevitably at odds with the Gospel of Jesus, who interrupted rather than fulfilled conventional certainties regarding God's will and plan for salvation. The promises of Christ flew in the face of tightly knit systems and precise expectations. Indeed, his very coming and cross were interruptive, disorienting in view of what was judged to be God's way and work in the world, summoning to a new order of things, in which pride of place is to be held by the last, littlest, lost, and least.

Those dismissed as postmodernists often display a strong passion for justice, especially justice for the marginal or excluded members of society who have been passed over in the process of human development.[3] Not only do they want justice for these peoples, groups, and individuals. They also want to make it possible for them to find their own voice and to develop their own creativity in serving a more equitable human world order. Orientations that draw on subterranean energies, as it were, are found in those who promote "green politics," in women's activities that break cultural moulds, in social movements of solidarity among the poor and with the poor, in small communities of faith and resistance, and in the reemergence of indigenous peoples as partners in building the future. Serving humanity cannot be an abstraction. It is located in communities of people and in movements of different sorts.

A trinitarian praxis theology certainly takes all these features of our common life into account and, in its appeal to Christian faith and ethic, seeks to enter into conversation with others even as it lives by the light of a revelation affirmed but never completely understood. It is concerned with a right development of the understanding of person. It knows that

---

[3] See, for example, Luc Ferry, *Man Made God: The Meaning of Life* (Chicago: University of Chicago Press, 2002).

it may be difficult to live out the mystery it professes as well as to attend to an authentic retrieval of what is said of Christ and God in the Scriptures. In its perspective on the communion of mortals and of mortals with earth, it follows the sacramental principle which finds all things suffused with the holiness of God. It asks for a good sacramental liturgy at the heart of the life of a Christian community and its ethical quest. Since language in its various kinds shapes existence, it knows that it has to be constantly attentive to language, its origins, its good and bad use, and its generative potential.

To understand what is happening within the church it is not enough to follow the debates of scholars. One has to turn, along with the above-cited David Tracy, to an orientation which comes to us from non-Western churches and which Tracy names the mystical-prophetic core of living the mystery of Christ and of doing theology. It is mystical because it attends to the contemplation of Jesus Christ, the one sent by God and endowed with the Spirit, in human life and in nature, and especially in the communities of the poor, in their suffering, their action, and their thirst for the kingdom of God. Without listening and attending to this presence which reveals itself in those who hear the Gospel and seek its signs in the world around them as they turn in hope to God in their suffering and bewilderment, a theology of God risks being stillborn, however erudite it may be. This trend is prophetic because it looks to life, to suffering, and to the quest for a common good with an eschatological orientation inspired by hearing the Scriptures. Further, it turns to Christ in his compassion in suffering and to the new life offered in the resurrection. This prophetic-mystical trend is buoyed by the energies of the Spirit who, in these last times, is poured out on all of God's people. This is an energy which is both understood and rejuvenated by a reading of the prophetic mission which Jesus of Nazareth, sent by the Spirit, takes unto himself and his disciples as he reads of the Jubilee in the prophet Isaiah while in the synagogue of Nazareth.

This mystical and prophetic quality of the Christian life that is pertinent to the quest for justice is fostered to a great extent by attention to Latin American theologians. It is, however, also strengthened by churches and scholars in Africa and Asia who have been able to integrate the religious perspectives of the peoples of these continents into their theologies, even as they struggle for a greater justice for their peoples in the widening global order. It is thus that Felix Wilfred of India sees in Jesus the "today" of the poor. As Jesus declared the prophecy of Isaiah to be fulfilled "today" in the hearing of the Galileans, so for Wilfred it is fulfilled "today," this day, in the poor of the world. This is because he contemplates Christ's life-giving presence among them, particularly among repressed minorities such as the *dalit*.[4] It is thus that Kwame Bediako knows Christ only when he sees him inserting himself almost in a new incarnation through the power of the Spirit into the oneness of African peoples with nature and with their ancestors, knowing that there can be no liberation and no justice for themselves except within this communion with the past and with the nature to which they remain beholden.[5]

Analyzing the Present: A Philosophical Insight

Though he himself considers dialogue with religion and theology a difficult project,[6] the thought of the philosopher Jürgen Habermas offers some insight into the present world situation. It can guide us in speaking of the Trinity in terms of making a life of authentic human development possible in a way that is attentive to particular expression while offering a large sense of communion within diversity. One of the more respected philosophers in Europe, he does not fear to speak of politics and political orders. He offers a fresh and practically oriented vision of the human person, the community, and society.[7] Instead of casting doubt on the gains of the age of the Enlightenment, Habermas offers a robust retrieval of its insights and objectives. Respecting its focus on the human and the personal, he finds this useful in freeing human persons and communities from the constraints of actual religious practice and the imposition of unnecessary universal absolutes that allow for no reasoning. He has proposed the norm of intersubjective communication as a way of drawing all persons into participation in the quest for the common good. The person neither lives nor is understood outside the workings of the intersubjective and only in this way may one come to a realization of authentic human potential. The possibility of a true, free, and fully participatory communication among persons has to be promoted and defended. This

[4] Felix Wilfred, *Margins: Site of Asian Theologies* (New Delhi: ISPCK, 2008).

[5] Kwame Bediako, *Jesus and the Gospel in Africa: History and Experience* (Maryknoll, NY: Orbis, 2000).

[6] See *Habermas, Modernity, and Public Theology*, ed. Don S. Browning and Francis Schüssler Fiorenza (New York: Crossroad, 1992), 226–50.

[7] The primary and secondary literature is massive, but for political implications, one could consult the small collection of essays, Jürgen Habermas, *The Liberating Power of Symbols*, Philosophical Essays, trans. by Peter Dew (Cambridge, MA: MIT Press, 2001).

is the framework of all human and social progress. The social critic and the politician who seek justice must therefore seek ways to guarantee intersubjective communication and action, offering a full participatory framework within which social, economic, and cultural life develops.

In explaining how he understands this, Habermas makes a distinction between "system" and "lifeworld." In the economic and political conditions of our present age, system refers to the market economy and the national and international apparatus within which it flourishes. The lifeworld is the immediate milieu of the individual social actor. In another age the lifeworld would respond to the authoritatively imposed modes of being and acting and value that made up the world in which all things were held together, including, of course, a normative religious practice. Today such normativity has been put into question. People, however, still look for clear signposts in their daily lives. More local discussion is needed to settle how a neighbourhood or a school system or a recreational facility is to be organized with the interests of all in mind. Diversity is in the current patterns of life and needs to be allowed in a civil way.

Within any larger system, people tend to act more directly on their immediate environment to make it habitable and responsive to pressing needs over which they may exercise some control. While Habermas believes that the understanding of political and economic systems (and we would say religious) must take this distinction into account, he opposes any analysis which disregards the interdependence of the lifeworld and the system in the negotiation of power. The goal of democratic societies is to allow persons and communities freedom and authority within their lifeworld, while also giving them participation in the shaping of systems, preventing any encroachment of the imperatives of system on areas of the lifeworld. For persons of faith, the question is whether religious belief and practice may be integral to both lifeworld and system, and indeed serve to mediate between the two, allowing for a conscious and informed participation at both levels.

In discussion with Joseph Ratzinger, now Pope Benedict XVI, Habermas has spoken of the contribution made by religion to civilization and even to the project of Modernity.[8] While still holding to the primacy of reason in communication and the construction of a world in which to live, he professes the need to draw on the rich resources of religious tra-

---

[8] Jürgen Habermas and Joseph Ratzinger, *The Dialectics of Secularization: On Reason and Religion* (San Francisco: Ignatius Press, 2007).

dition. He maintains that Sacred Scriptures and religious traditions have preserved, over millennia, intuitions about the sources of error and about redemption that are necessary to the outcome of human striving. Religious expression and the pursuit of religious virtue allow for a number of sensitivities, nuances, and modes of expression that the efforts of human reason alone do not provide. The focus on personal human rights is not a sufficient ground on which to build a society in which humans may flourish. There is also a set of perceptions and values that are concerned with the nature of persons "to be with" and, indeed, not simply being with one another but being with all that is in nature and cosmos, a being with the other that necessarily entails a "being for." Politics, ethics, and law are not three realms that exist alongside each other. They penetrate each other and their right exercise needs an anthropology which takes the human fully into account, or takes into account the full human. Reason alone does not present this humanity, but other forms of relating and expressing have to work with it.

It is particularly in the domain of symbolic expression and what this brings to the amplitude of human life that religious tradition provides much that is needed in any common human endeavour. Like Ratzinger, Habermas often focuses on the larger picture when discussing religion, but the discussion itself of religious expression has to account for living within the immediacy of life's constraints and possibilities, as well as within a larger world. Symbolism of any kind, including religious, has to function well within both worlds and should serve to mediate between the two.

Writing of politics and economics, Habermas asks persistently how the two concerns interrelate and interact. He points to the importance of the reality and role of particular human communities and their specific identities. When the present quest for a world order is dominated by market forces or the imposition of a uniform and universal ideal of governance and participation, human community in its more immediate and practical realities suffers and the identities of persons, communities, and cultures are put at risk. This does not mean that we are to embrace an anachronistic vision of closed communities. For genuine progress in the way of peace and justice, people themselves need the supports which give them the cognitive and creative power to shape their lifeworlds and to take part in the development and working of larger political and economic systems. The lives of small communities need as much care as the commonwealth. If those of faith persuasion are responsive to these insights, they will ask how faith enables this quest and, in the name of the transcendent, offers insight, persuasion, and value that goes beyond the Enlightenment's convictions even while embracing many of its specific gains. This would be more constructive than finding in the church the last bastion of truth and the bulwark that stands firm against the onslaughts of relativism, consumerism, and hedonism.

In creating the lifeworld, and in mediating between system and lifeworld, symbols, rites, and all forms of aesthetic expression have a vital role in all areas of human life. The symbolic or the poetic is a way of perceiving and a means of relating. It opens up a vision of total reality, where all things are interrelated in a sense of the whole, while respecting the being of particular entities, be these persons, communities, or things. It is symbolic expression which gives the possibility of seeing the present in relation to both past and future, and of seeing each particular event or reality within the whole. Symbolic networks are necessary to the sense of community and the identity of peoples, nations, and religious bodies as they offer a way of seeing reality and of finding one's place within it.

Implications for Living the Gospel: Focus on Local Community

The more we see the connection between cultural perceptions of reality, social and economic systems, and the exigencies of local habitat, the more urgent the matter of participatory intersubjective communications becomes. The more we see how injustice affects every aspect of human life, the more we see the need for a conversation and an interaction which befriends the local as well as the global. It is a pressing challenge to the preaching and inculturation of the Gospel and to theology to find their place within this broadly conceived concern.

The implications of the distinction between local and global in the service of a just world order emerge when we consider the position of particular peoples within the global economy, or within a globalization that is driven by economics as the governing, if not sole, concern. An especially important and telling example is that of indigenous peoples in different parts of the world. Their life world is disrupted, their relation to social and political systems ambiguous, and their voices seldom heard in national and international communication and planning.

Some of the difficulties and aspirations of the position of these peoples were spelled out at a meeting in Baguio, Philippines, sponsored by the World Council of Churches in 2009.[9] Representatives from the Americas, from Africa and Asia, and from Nordic European countries were present at this meeting. In understandings of development, central importance needs to be given to what is happening to those affected by "development." First of all, the immediate environment has been destroyed for many communities, or they have been uprooted from it. As the concluding statement of the meeting puts it, "The land, the mountains, the deserts, the rivers and forests have been the home and life-sustaining resources of indigenous people for centuries. But today, they are being misused and raped to meet the growing demands of consumerism." It is pointed out that the power of the earth to sustain and nourish life is being destroyed, at great cost to the environment itself and with enormous human and social consequences. Second, with this the identity of communities is at risk, for land is fundamental to their existence as particular peoples, not only for sustenance, but also for the expression and maintenance of their culture.

Unfortunately, throughout history disrespect for this identity has been inherent to foreign conquest of territories. Therefore, the Baguio report states: "To be able to chart one's own destiny based on traditional economic, political and socio-cultural systems and processes—within the framework of unity, justice and genuine development—is a naming, self-identifying process. However, it is necessary to emphasize the point that self-identification and self-determination are community processes and must be guarded against bourgeois individualistic interests."

With this in view, the values that are learned from indigenous peoples as foundational for development are enunciated: community over individual interests; a logic of relationality or interconnection between all living beings, even inanimate beings such as rocks and sites; simple functionality over luxury, involving a respectful and reciprocal attitude to and use of natural resources; redefinition of power and status, not based on the accumulation of wealth and dominance over others.

Those taking part in the WCC-sponsored meeting were attentive to the religious aspect of development, noting that the religious vision of these peoples is disturbed because with destruction of the environment,

---

[9] *Report from the International Consultation on the Ecclesial and Social Visions of the Indigenous Peoples*, accessible at www.oikoumene.org/en/documents/wcc -programmes/unity-mission-evangelism-and-spirituality/just-and-inclusive -communities/indigenous-people.

its symbolic expression is disrupted. What this means for living the Gospel is that much that belongs to traditional religious expression has to be reinstated, such as respect for sacred sites and a reverence for the earth and cosmos born of a lived communion between humans and other beings. Ritual, stories, foundational myths, utopias are all tied up with relation to the environment. Grounding the Gospel in culture means integrating what they express. In the Baguio report one indigenous group puts it this way: "Our storytelling is our struggle, and to listen to them or construct rituals around them is a re-assertion of who we are. In our myths, we give an account of our origins and destiny, our past and the future we hope for in the midst of our painful lives."

In spelling out their spiritual and theological vision, Christian communities among indigenous peoples do so in dialogue with their own traditions and ancestors. At the meeting in Baguio, elements of this vision were enunciated which are recovered in all that follows in this volume: the understanding of Pasch as a liberation of slaves and the founding of a people deeply embedded in the earth; the constant practice of Jubilee among the Jewish people for the redress of wrongs to the land and to the poor; the beginning of the mission of Jesus in the recall of the prophetic text that embodies this Jubilee perspective; the need to see Jesus himself in his own indigenous setting in order to understand what he preached and even the mode of his crucifixion and then what is promised in his resurrection and the sending of the Spirit; a reading of Genesis and Wisdom on creation so as to see how harmonious needs to be the relation between humanity and the environment and so as to address ecological responsibilities.

The concern for doing justice does not look primarily to those whose basic wants are met but to those who suffer discrimination in well-sustained societies and to the millions who are subject to immense suffering. All believers have to take stock of the suffering of whole nations, races, classes, indeed, of whole peoples and to respond to the call to heal wounds, not just of individual persons, but of the earth and all the living. This taking stock has to start by attending to how these peoples themselves may be able to find hope in their own lives and to the forces which enable them to live a more truly human life. With a better sense of a global communion and of communion with creation, peoples can search together for the proper disposition and distribution of material goods in a world whose economic engines are near exhaustion, indeed, on the verge of complete collapse. Yet still they manage to drive millions into the squalor that breeds disease and fuels violence.

There is always a tendency to see sin and its remedy in the hearts of individual beings. But nowadays especially it is impossible to talk of seeking justice in the name of God without realizing the extent to which we live within sinful structures, that we ourselves are party to a system of injustice and sin against the neighbor and against God's works in the cosmos. It is this sensitivity that prompts us to respond more fully to the need for forgiveness and reconciliation, that "purification of memories" to which John Paul II called the church in preparation for the great Jubilee 2000. Knowing that God made visible the divine presence in the world in the midst of suffering, that of the enslaved people of Israel and that of Jesus Christ in his solidarity with the suffering, alerts us to the fact that the quest for God that is a common quest has to find a starting point for today within the circles of suffering. We are not onlookers. We are participants. Even as the church engages in a new self-reflection, open to the temporal world and to other religions, it is from its faith in the triune God present in the world that it finds the reason for its own presence, engaged with humility, in the midst of persons, communities, and peoples in our own times. This faith allows Christian believers to speak with meaning and hope of the origin and destiny of human life, of what constitutes the good life, of what gives meaning and purpose to human behaviour, in personal quest and in the quest for a common good that embraces all peoples as they live out their lives on this earth. A lived, practical belief in the Trinity enables believers to discern the vital forces which are at work in human life, and to give them their orientation in the pursuit of meaning and value as they work together with others toward a more just and humane world order. This at a moment when human communities are faced with dehumanizing forces that rip them apart and divorce them from the earth to which they belong.

Signs of Divine Advent

In light of all the above, theology requires that we return to the expression "signs of the times." When *Gaudium et Spes* used this term, it meant that the church needed to be attentive to those features of contemporary life and society that are indicative of the present and possible future of humanity. This use of the expression was already criticized during the council by some of the Protestant observers who wanted the council to turn to the biblical use of the phrase for purposes of discernment. Since the council, Catholic commentators have taken up this criticism, noting that it is not enough to understand the times in terms of what is most symptomatic of social and cultural life. We need a means of discerning the presence of God in this. But this requires more than an application of given doctrines that serve as criteria for judgment. What, one may ask, are the signs of God's advent and promise in the midst of our human striving?

In light of that sign of the advent of God's kingdom, which is the sign of Jonah (Matt 16:1-4 with Matt 12:38-40), reading those signs that give insight into present reality entails looking to those places where suffering is most intense but where hope lives. What Jesus says of the sign of Jonah could be related to the signs that, according to Matthew, were shown in the story of the death of Jesus (Matt 27:45-54). Though these signs may not be taken as literal account, they tell us that wherever the kingdom advents there are signs that the death of Jesus overcomes death, that religious systems cannot hold this back, and that, even when faced with death, some—like the centurion—will see in the death of the innocent one a testimony to God the Father and to the promise of life. We are always compelled to search for such signs among victims and those who stand with them, to see how the hope for life prevails even in the hour of death. They are woven into the testimony of a people as the gospel story is told, so that we see as gospel stories the works and death of Martin Luther King; Oscar Romero; the Jesuits of El Salvador, their housekeeper, and her daughter; those who lived the love of their (ethnic) enemies during the genocide of Rwanda; and the Jews who celebrated the Sabbath in concentration camps among those who, in Primo Levi's terms, seemed deprived of humanity itself.[10]

Signs of the kingdom in its making can also be found in the practitioners of the Beatitudes. We know of the presence of the Spirit and of the rule of God in the peacemakers, in those who gladly suffer persecution for Christ's sake, in the suffering who keep their trust in God and support one another in loving compassion, and in communities of the poor who, in listening to the Word of God, work together to achieve a fuller development of their lives.

In this way, while we see the forces at work which bring about human degradation, we also see signs of new life born of a suffering by which people allow themselves to be alerted to human need, to action in com-

---

[10] See, for example, Primo Levi, *If This Is a Man* (Oxford: Abacus, 2003).

munity, to a new sense of solidarity as the basis for action. Even a short rendering of what peoples suffer and of the causes of suffering gives some sense of where to look for God's presence and action in the world whereby a true order of justice may be forged. In taking stock of their suffering, we see how oppressed or marginalized groups aspire to a new place in society, groups such as indigenous peoples, women of many cultures, gay and lesbian people, and immigrant populations. Indeed, as the world awakens to the poverty and exploitation of peoples, it also awakens to the twinning of the exploitation of humans and the exploitation of the natural resources of earth. There is an imbalance in the ways in which persons and peoples are left marginal to a social order, but it is an imbalance which may be set aright from within the circles of the suffering when they take cognizance of the dignity given them by nature and by divine gift. From within their suffering they find the inspiration for leading a fuller human life that matters to others and indeed to world order, and for offering this knowledge and hope to all of us. For many outside these circles, but still ready to live a life of solidarity in a common quest, there is indeed the inspiration of the *kenosis* of Jesus Christ which means concretely a readiness to consent to the death of familiar life-forms, of inherited traditions, secular and religious, which, while comfortable to them, turn out to be oppressive of others.

The signs of the times sought in this evangelical sense are not sought in a world different from the signs intended in *Gaudium et Spes* when the conciliar members spoke of looking for what gives us insight into the human world and in cultures. They show up in the same realities. They indicate that within all human social and cultural developments there are present those movements of divine grace and divine love which lead to a fuller and more just ordering of reality.

With these considerations in mind, we can look to the revelation of the Trinity as the ground of a Christian ethic of justice, where the order of love and the order of justice converge. In treating of virtue Christian theologians must of necessity say that in the Christian dispensation love is the form of all the virtues. Justice itself, with its concern for good order and the well-being of all beings, collective and individual, is subsumed by charity, as Benedict XVI has reminded us in the encyclical *Caritas in Veritate*. In face of sin and the call for forgiveness, we are given an order of love which is an order of mercy, that order which is restored through the sacrifice of Christ. In evangelical perspective the norm of equity is the abundance of divine mercy written into the ways of human life on earth.

Paradoxically, in the quest for a universal order of justice, it is with particular, local communities that we must begin. When we attend to the structures of suffering, we see that the divine presence and inspiration is found first and foremost in particular communities and we see why the church in its social ethic gives support to local, traditional, and indigenous communities. Indeed, when addressing economic realities in certain areas of its teaching, the episcopacy has adopted the language of building sustainable local communities, seeing these as most suited to preserving and fostering an integrated human life.[11] This vision must be articulated in view of the historical facts with which we live, currents which, whatever their advantages, call for a greater appreciation for regionality, locality, and diversity among persons and communities so that lifeworld communities, each with its own sense of origins and destiny, might flourish. This entails greater respect for what is understood to constitute the good life in diverse lifeworlds, as well as the diversity of symbols that function in these communities.

In the development of the larger, multinational structures which globalization has brought, local, smaller groups and communities must still be respected. Openness to the gift of the life of God given through Word and Spirit offers a way that is able to free persons and communities to live in communion with one another, living from and for the gift of God's love in a way that brings about a deeper communion which respects local and regional difference, cultural specificity, and traditional values, whether religious or not.

An ethic rooted in the descent of divine gift in the life of a people allows fuller life and human flourishing to come to form, to stand forth. Such an ethic attentive to the descent of the divine gift of life into the world and, more particularly, into the world of the suffering has its foundation in an understanding of the divine primarily as the source of life rather than primarily as authority or domin(ion)ation. Such an ethic is not easily harnessed by simply fulfilling the requirements of distributive justice but has to include the discernment of injustice that opens the space to acts of forgiveness, reconciliation, and redress. This ethic cannot be imposed by authority, however much it is guided by a

---

[11] For example, *At Home in the Web of Life: A Pastoral Message on Sustainable Communities in Appalachia* (Webster Springs, WV: Catholic Communities of Appalachia, 1995); CELAM, *V Conferencia General, Aparecida 2007, Documento Conclusivo* (Bogota: Centro de Publicaciones CELAM, 2008).

plausible exercise of it. It is not to be seen as a biblically conceived order of human life, history, the world, and all in it, which is then superimposed on persons in diverse lifeworlds in their quest for the authentically human, in their desire to live freely their own sense of meaning, purpose, and value, in their struggle to make good on life. Rather, an ethic that is made known as an invitation in the descent of divine gift is discerned through conversation and active communication which privileges the needs, the requirements, the voices of the poor and suffering. It can even find ways of cooperation with the concerns of the more secularly minded whose hearts are open to every dimension of life, both human and nonhuman, and who consciously set out in pursuit of an authentic human development for all citizens of the world.

Such an ethic stands forth first and foremost in the witness of the children of God who testify to the cross and to its promise of freedom, making of their own bodies the seedbed of their highest hope. It is in their testimony that the *kenosis* of God is shining forth, shimmering in weakness and vulnerability, summoning to an *agape* which comes to full form in a reconfiguration of justice as it is commonly understood, and in a love that moves us toward the transcendent that is itself to be known in the striving of a people who live by hope amid oppression, suffering, and despair. We see too how sacramental liturgy finds its place at the heart of such an ethic, for it is there that Christian communities open their hearts and minds to the indwelling of God in trinitarian communion. Speaking about the Divine Trinity is possible only because we are caught up in this ineffable mystery. Inspired by worship itself as well as by the Scriptures, we know the role of apophatic reserve in face of divine mystery, lest we speak as those who do not still have to await a fullness of revelation and a continued generous outpouring of divine life befitting those who live and have their being in eschatological hope. Within such a hope we act with a firm conviction of the inspiring force of a divine dispensation of grace and gift.

As far as the practice of religion is concerned, or the ways in which Christians insert themselves into the life of humankind, we can say that religious outlook and practice related to the Trinity would meet the criteria for the role of religion in global society formulated for example by the Princeton University political scientist Richard Falk.[12] Falk considers

---

[12] Richard Falk, *Human Rights Horizons: The Pursuit of Justice in a Globalizing World* (London: Routledge, 2000).

the development of religion within the overall growth of society, but Christian practice may be seen to correspond to these criteria. For him, it can be said that at their best religions offer a significant contribution when they allow for the following: (1) they take suffering seriously and respond to real people who suffer; (2) they attend to the roots of popular culture; (3) they anchor an ethos of solidarity; (4) they provide normative horizons based on a transcendent ethic; (5) they rely on the power of faith and hope to overcome pessimism; (6) they foster a sense of human limits and fallibility; (7) they provide identity in a world that has lost its mooring; (8) they work for justice and reconciliation. To this could be added the role of religion in helping people find their place within a cultural expression that respects their own lifeworld, or the immediacy of their sense of place and time. It is our wager that appealing to faith in the mystery of the Trinity, with attention to both tradition and current realities, may respond to this public role of religion and to the need for cultural specificity and diversity within the one communion or body of the faithful, while allowing for a credible witness to human solidarity and providing inspiration for common action. With this in view and with what has been said in the introduction, we turn to an overview of currents in the theology of the Trinity that relate especially to praxis.

Conclusion

In light of the above, four things come to the fore in working on a trinitarian theology which serves as foundation on which to build a new order of justice inspired by divine bounty.[13] First, the situation in the world today calls for greater respect for local and culturally specific communities, for while the world evolves on a global scale, such peoples should not be condemned to extinction. Second, Christian communities come to know the glory of God in an authentic social *agapic* action that, in the name of divine wisdom, strives to transform ecclesial, cultural, and social horizons and values. This action embraces the victims of history and human technology in compassion and heeds their voices and their cries as a divine word speaking from within suffering. Third, Christian communities that seek their prophetic place in human life have to inte-grate the cognitive and affective desires and expectation which they find

---

[13] See David N. Power, "Liturgical Praxis: A New Consciousness at the Eye of Worship," in *Worship: Culture and Theology* (Washington, DC: Pastoral Press, 1990), 140.

in all persons and peoples, seeing therein the seeds of a divine longing that knows only eschatological fulfilment in communion with the glory of God. Fourth, there has to be a keen appreciation of the symbolic and what it conveys of a vision of the order of things at the heart of praxis. This emerges and finds ever-new expression among those who live by the presence and promise of the Beatitudes of the gospel as this shows forth first in Christ, then in his Spirit-filled church, and then among those who live by another name for God but among whom we can find what in Christian speech we would call the seeds of the Word and the breath of the Spirit.

Suggested Readings

Suggested readings are provided after each chapter of this volume. This brief listing is not a bibliography for all that has been presented in the chapter. It is a suggestion of readings that could be useful to readers wanting to follow up on the particular theme of a trinitarian praxis of justice.

Lamb, Matthew. *Solidarity with Victims: Toward a Theology of Social Transformation.* New York: Crossroad, 1982.
This is a helpful treatment of a praxis approach to theology and society.

Lane, Dermot. *Foundations for Social Theory, Praxis, Process and Salvation.* Mahwah, NJ: Paulist, 1984.
This is a good overview of the relation between theory, practice, and social change in a theology of salvation.

Sanks, T. Howland, and John Coleman. *Reading the Signs of the Times: Resources for Social and Cultural Analysis.* Mahwah, NJ: Paulist, 1993.
A sociologist's take on reading the signs of the times in the present era.

Tracy, David. "On Naming the Present." *Concilium: On the Threshold of the Third Millennium* no. 1 (1990): 66–85.
This is an excellent survey from a theological perspective of the place of the church in relation to Modernity and postmodernity.

CHAPTER 2

Theologies of Trinity
Related to Praxis

If a theology of the Trinity is to guide the quest for justice and peace, it has to be seen as a theology that relates to practice, not only in a general way, but in a way that is pertinent to the current globalization of human society. Having considered this, in this chapter we review theologies that are open to a praxis consideration.

Given currents of globalization and massive economic breakdown on the world scene, the revelation of the Trinity through its working in human life offers both practical guidelines and religious symbolism that gather different aspects of communal life into one. It offers hope for peoples and communities striving for human flourishing while immersed in diverse lifeworlds with their own practices and community identity, those who are often besieged by needs and wants which are hard to meet. Each people may seem to have its own distinctive sense of origins and destiny and to express it through different stories, rituals, and symbols. Nevertheless, it is possible that a shared symbolism, allowing for an internal diversity of expression, may draw the many into an inspiring vision. This can mobilize particular and local communities to live in the world in such a way that they can come together and stand against the tide of those negative currents of globalization which risk obliterating a true sense of communion because of its all too materialistic vision of the human good.

Historical Ways of Presenting the Trinity

Historical inquiry makes it clear that an understanding of the mystery of the Trinity has always had to bring together a sense of how each of the three—Father, Son, and Spirit—is distinct and yet all three are united in one communion. It also makes it clear that from early times teachers have seen Christian life as a participation in this mystery of communion, made approachable through the incarnation of the Word and the gift of the Holy Spirit.

Theologies of the Trinity are better appreciated when it is seen how they relate to the times in which they emerged. The conciliar constitution *Gaudium et Spes* brought the Catholic Church out of a prolonged period of antimodernistic aggression in an effort to collaborate with others in the building of a new order where justice and peace become a common quest. To offer a process which allows for a better understanding of the world, in its positive and negative realities, it spoke of isolating and reading the signs of the times, that is, the indicators which give insight into what is happening as the world proceeds along its given way. Faith communities and theologians in different times and places have struggled to do just this, to read the signs of their own times as expressive of needs and aspirations and values espoused. Theologians have worked, often in very unsystematic fashion, with a fundamental insight, a governing concern, to meet the needs and urgent demands of their age. In every age, in light of their here and now, in response to questions engaged, theologians have given shape to distinctive approaches to questions of human origin and destiny guided by a central intuition about Jesus Christ, enlightened by a particular image or understanding of Christ.

Whether looking at Justin or Origen, or especially Irenaeus or Athanasius, it must be recognized that their theological writing was done with pastoral intent in the face of new questions, in light of shifting modes of perceiving and being. Athanasius' preeminent concern with the incarnation, that God had spoken and is speaking in human flesh, included a sustained argument against any effort to denigrate human flesh. Centuries later, in face of a society knowing new developments and a new consciousness of what constitutes the person, Aquinas guided reflection along the curve of an *exitus et reditus* where all is perceived as coming from God and going back to God, with providence ordering all things according to what pertains to their particular mode of being and acting. The wisdom of God known though faith in Christ and aided by reason was the key to living the Christian life as much as it was the inspiration of theological thought.

For the followers of Francis, including Thomas' contemporary, Bonaventure, the focus was on the following and imitation of Christ in his abandonment to poverty and in his love of the poor, even as these were known in those who profited not at all from changes in society and its economic workings. The symbol in which Christ and the poor were drawn together was the legend of *il poverello*, Francis of Assisi, whose flesh made manifest Christ crucified in his here and now. Centuries later, in the post-Enlightenment world, the Tübingen School looked for a way of understanding the human person in the light of Christ and of the mystery of the Trinity, which would enable Christians to take their part in the forming of a new social order rather than stepping outside it. This effort was, in fact, aided by developments in scriptural studies, which brought new appreciation of how God's revelation was formed and how it addresses human life.

In what follows, we give a brief outline of some theologies of the past that have importance for contemporary theologians as they consider historical inquiry in the light of present needs, and the ways in which knowledge of the divine mystery influences thought about social arrangements.

First, there are the models that, in the East more clearly than in the West, situate the mystery of the Divine Trinity within the context of liturgical worship, something which of itself demands *ascesis* in the whole of life and care for the other in order to ready oneself for worship. Of particular note is the work of the Cappadocians with the attention given to *perichoresis* as a way of expressing the nature of the interpenetrating relationship of Father, Son/Word, and Spirit. Contemporary theological efforts to retrieve the importance of *perichoresis* in light of its potential for social reform do not always do justice to the liturgical mooring of this notion. Christian prayer and worship, indeed all Christian living, originates in and is directed to the Father, through the Word/Son, in the Spirit. *Perichoresis* in the Greek understanding means the communion of Father, Word, and Spirit shown forth in the economy, that is, the divine dispensation, of the saving works of God in history. This is, to some measure, expressive of the fullness of the divine life. But such recognition requires that even as the presence of divine gifts is seen the eternal mystery is considered as beyond intellectual reach, approached only through the obedience and submission expressed in doxology.

This apophatic reserve needs to be given its due in contemporary retrievals of the insights of the Cappadocians into divine *perichoresis* in efforts to construct models for personal, interpersonal, and social relationships. The communion of the Three in One in equal, mutual, reciprocal, and interdependent relationship is known to us only as we participate in it through the mission of Word and Spirit, or through their presence in our lives.

The followers of Gregory Palamas in his reading of the Cappadocians find that an apophatic and doxological approach to our share in the mystery of the Trinity is best respected by seeing the presence of the three and human transformation brought about by the divine energies of the three, rather than through direct entry into the divinity. Due attention must also be given to the patristic conviction about the order/*taxis* of Father, Son, and Spirit,[1] or to the relationship between Word and Spirit, which is understood in such a way as to see that it is known through the Spirit shining forth in the Word and the Father's Word spoken in the Breath/ing of the Spirit. One of the complaints about Western liturgy is that, unlike that of the East, it has often focused on the sending of the Son and on the mediation of the Son without attending to the communication and action of the Spirit. Attending to the three as known in the ways in which they are present to us, and by which in action and prayer and worship we live by and within their mediation, gives us a framework for advancing human communion in the name of the triune God.

A second model from Christian history, to which some contemporary theology looks for insight, is that which emerges from the Victorine School as it carries over into the theology of Bonaventure. Here, the focus is on the relationship, the communion, of Father and Son which necessitates a third, which/who is the bond of love between Father and Son/Word. Contemporary approaches to understanding the Trinity such as that of Jürgen Moltmann and, to a lesser degree, of Catherine Mowry LaCugna, which emphasize uniqueness, particularity, and diversity reflective of the "three-ness" of Father, Son/Word, and Spirit, carry forward the insights of this historical model in an effort to apply them in contemporary social and ecclesial contexts.

The third model of thought, which is most prominent in Western Christian theology, is that which was developed in the works of Augustine and Aquinas. Here, the focus is on the mission of the Word and Spirit, and the analogy with intellect and love, word and action, which

---

[1] In his construction of a trinitarian model of social relations as corrective to social inequality and injustice, Jürgen Moltmann maintains that the *monarche* of the Father is at the root of the problem of social and other manifestations of inequality and injustice. He proposes that the *taxis*, or order of the three persons, might just a well be that of Spirit, Son, Father, or Son, Spirit, Father, or Son, Father, Spirit, or Spirit, Father, Son.

serves to give insight and to grasp their presence in human life. The truth of the one God is made manifest in the mission of the Word and the Spirit, revealed through the Divine Names of Father, Son/Word, and Spirit. When the term "person" is invoked, it is to emphasize that each is distinct in relationship, though fully divine, and that even this distinction and oneness can be understood only somewhat by attending to what is most spiritual to our knowledge, namely, actions of knowing and loving. As Karl Rahner has pointed out very clearly, this has nothing to do with modern notions of person with their assertions of personal autonomy.

Contemporary Western Theologies

In looking for the implications of the revelation of the Divine Trinity for our current desire for justice, we may ask how contemporary quests for God relate to contemporary realities and concerns. One could, of course, limit the question to the field of Christology. There, we indeed find how authors responded to various insights into the human person and community. Karl Rahner's governing concern was a recovery of the humanity of Christ as key to understanding the divine communion in which all human beings have a share. Taking his cue from John 17, Yves Congar's overarching concern was with the church as the one Body of Christ in an ecumenical setting. For Hans Urs von Balthasar, Christ's *kenosis* and his descent among the dead, the divine self-emptying, provided a key to understanding the mystery of Christ.[2] Liberation theologies, for their part, seek the presence and understanding of Christ among communities of the marginal and especially of the poor.

Alongside developments in Christology, there are, maybe less developed, new currents in pneumatology, especially as Western thought meets Eastern, currents that show there is no adequate understanding of Christ without associating his mission with the mission of the Holy Spirit. As a result of these theological currents, there is a better understanding of the church, its inner life and its apostolic mandate to bring Christ to the world in virtue of the presence of Word and Spirit. It was in writing of the baptized faithful that the Second Vatican Council pointed a way

---

[2] In his encyclical *Fides et Ratio* 92–99, John Paul II spells out what he sees as the "current tasks for theology." He maintains that the prime task of theology is "understanding God's *kenosis*," and, by implication, that the image of the self-emptying of God in Christ, the divine self-abandon, is the most apt christological image for our own time and place.

to know how Christ and Spirit are present in the human world and in all the workings of human society. With the constitution of the Pontifical Council for Justice and Peace and the fostering of interlocked entities of this sort across the globe, the questions about Christ and about Spirit began to take form also as questions about peace and justice.

Turning to the question of diverse understandings of the Trinity, their consequences for social order are best understood when they are seen to emerge in response to different realities faced by persons, communities, and societies of the post-Enlightenment world. The desire for justice is never a given but always finds new expression in the hour of suffering and need. And so it is also for the question of God. It is indeed when there seems to be no exit to suffering, or when the church responds inadequately to it, that people begin to reckon with what they describe as their loss of faith. Is it ever possible to pronounce the name of God in affliction?

Karl Barth and Karl Rahner

We do not pretend to give an extensive presentation of these two theologians, but our aim is to place them in their historical context, finding this pertinent to an understanding of the order of justice prompted by reflection on the divine mystery. Both theologies emerged when a response was sought to suffering and the quest for a place for God, for the transcendent, in the forging of a viable human future. Karl Barth was witness to the sufferings and dissolutions of society between the Wars and in the aftermath of World War II and to the failures of churches to speak and to witness in difficult times. Aware that theological discourse, both Protestant and Catholic, had often used language about God and divine attributes quite inadequately in an inadequate response to God's Word, he wanted to develop a trinitarian theology that would speak of the God of revelation in human existence and in human history. Hence the theology of the triune God needed to be more securely anchored in the biblical revelation, in the Word of God proclaimed.

Barth knew the havoc which a reliance on human reason and human invention could wreak. He resisted too the inroads of reason in historical reconstructions of the Scriptures and retrieval of the events of revelation as historical inquiry could unveil them. At the same time, he resisted what he saw as the Catholic response to Modernity, namely, recourse to an innate knowledge of the natural law as God's law and a use of the analogy of being to construct a metaphysics of revelation. He called for a total openness to the Word of God, to Christ as the revelation of God, and to the work of the Spirit in guiding the understanding of this revelation. Understanding the justice of God means starting with divine mercy. Humanity is locked into its sinful conditions, incapable of saving itself and incapable of any true knowledge of God. Revelation is the self-unveiling of God given to humankind, where God reveals himself in Jesus Christ as Lord. In his eternal reality, God will ever remain veiled, but he is so free that he can manifest himself in temporal form. This does not mean that humans can grasp God by using analogies, but in revelation God approaches humans in such a way that they can acknowledge divine sovereignty and mercy and follow him in following Jesus Christ in whom he is revealed. In the course of writing a dogmatics which relies solely on the Word of God, Barth had occasion to question the use of contemporary notions of person in writing of the inner life of the Trinity of Father, Word, and Spirit and suggested that to be true to the unknowability of the God who remains hidden even in revelation, it might be better to speak of three modes of being, as these are known in revelation.

Barth devoted a considerable portion of the first volume of his *Church Dogmatics* to a treatment of the doctrine of the Trinity.[3] With attention to the Word Revealed who is the Son and the Word Revealing who is the Spirit, Barth helped shift the prevailing focus on the Trinity away from speculation about the intradivine life of three persons—the so-called immanent Trinity—to God's self-revelation in the economy of redemption, that is, to the saving works of God in history.

Barth's opposition to use of the analogy of being in discourse on God is important to the development of his own theology and to subsequent theologies, Protestant and Catholic alike. To see the nature of his protest, it is necessary to keep the time frame in mind. Barth wished to avoid metaphysical language. He found that theologies in circulation left God indifferent in his own being to the work of creation and redemption. Catholic theology at the time presented God as the necessary being, the one who above all beings is *causa sui*, dependent on nothing else, yet the highest in a chain of being and causality that leaves all being and all action dependent on him. God is present everywhere but untouched in the divine inner life. In this context,

---

[3] Karl Barth, *Church Dogmatics*, a selection and introduction by Helmut Gollwitzer. (Louisville/London: Westminster John Knox, 1994; first published Edinburgh: T &T Clark, 1961).

speculation on the mystery of the Trinity remained abstract and left divine works out of consideration, which, of course, resulted in two distinct academic treatises dealing separately of the one God and of the triune God. The liberal response of Deism was unsatisfactory to Barth because it affirmed God as Creator but then thought of God as indifferent to the world he had made, leaving humans their complete autonomy. The turn to the Word and the biblical narration was needed in face of such distortions of the divine.

The God present in the revealed Word Incarnate and in the revealing Spirit given to the world is known in his merciful and compassionate presence to his works. God's freedom is indeed to be asserted, but it is the freedom of self-determination. Barth wished to avoid the arbitrary notions of God's works and commands inherent to Nominalism, which allowed for a capricious, indeed, fickle God while still affirming God's sovereign freedom. Creation and redemption are choices, not necessities, but they are acts of self-determination, an overflowing of divine goodness into the life of the world and the life of redeemed humanity.

Karl Rahner also thought it necessary, despite patristic and dogmatic theology, to distance theology somewhat from speaking of Divine Person. This is because revelation cannot integrate the modern notion of autonomous and self-evolving human person into a notion of Divine Being and communion. He was concerned with the loss of the power of established God language for a humanity and a Christian people in the throes of secularization, when societies could no longer, as in "religious" times, be built on a vision of a Creator and Ruler God to whom all authority, both religious and temporal, owed allegiance. Therefore, careful not to allow speech about God to be subject to a secular discourse on the human person, he restored a perspective on the theology of the Trinity which started with the scriptural discourse on Christ and Spirit and with the spiritual experience, of persons and communities, of God as Word and God as Spirit. One could no longer tolerate theological, ethical, and catechetical teaching which spoke of obedience to God in the philosophical language of monotheism while leaving the mystery of the Trinity in the dustbin of the impenetrable, asking only for a submission of mind and heart to the existence of divine mystery, making sure simply that the language was orthodox, however shallow the understanding may be. Hence a theology of God needed to be related to experience, of both heart and mind, and to offer a trinitarian and eschatological vision of God's self-communication and salvific action in the world.

Rahner's assertion that the economic Trinity (God revealed in history) *is* the immanent Trinity (the unfathomable mystery of God) and vice versa—often called "Rahner's rule"—drew attention, especially in Roman Catholic theological circles, to the presence and action of God in salvation history as point of departure for whatever might be known or said of the triune life.[4] The God who communicates in Word and Spirit in the economy of salvation is the very God who lives for all eternity in the Divine Communion of Father, Son/Word, and Spirit. There are not two trinities but one: the God who is. This is the God who is with us and for us in the grand economy of salvation.

With the formulation of Rahner's rule, talk of the Trinity became more central to the conversation of a wide range of Christian theologians, a conversation that continues today. A governing concern was and remains the conviction that what has often been thought to be a doctrine with little consequence for the day in and day out of Christian life is in fact the very ground and substance *of* Christian life and practice, both within faith communities and within the world order of which they are a part.

Catherine Mowry LaCugna was much indebted to Karl Rahner, working out some of the social consequences of his writings. While there is no explicit recognition of this, her theology is not unlike that of Bonaventure and the Victorines whose emphasis on the relationship of Father and Son necessitates a third. The appeal of LaCugna's interpersonal or social model in working out a social ethic is clear, since it sees the three in communion as both model and agent of the kingdom of God. Here, the Trinity is thought to be a model for patterning human relationship based on the equality, mutuality, and interdependence of the Three who are God. The advantages of this model are many, but care needs to be taken to avoid easy slippage into a highly anthropomorphic view of the three persons and a reading into the divine life of a social agenda of equality for all persons. What is called for in appealing to this model is a clear sense of apophatic reserve in making claims about modelling social arrangements on what is claimed to be the nature of the relationship of the Three who are One. While emphasizing the interpersonal and social implications of the doctrine in her *God for Us*,[5] LaCugna gives considerable attention to the liturgical mooring of the insights of the

---

[4] Karl Rahner, *The Trinity* (London: Burns & Oates, 1970).

[5] Catherine Mowry LaCugna, *God for Us: The Trinity and Christian Life* (San Francisco: Harper, 1991).

Eastern traditions, particularly those of the Cappadocians whom she favors. Her work also demonstrates apophatic reserve in her refusal to engage in speculation about the precise structure of the intradivine life, the so-called immanent Trinity. LaCugna maintains that before this ineffable mystery, the only appropriate response is the doxology that gives way to silence.

Jürgen Moltmann and Dorothee Soelle

Subsequent to Barth's and Rahner's turn to the Trinity in a recovery of a language about God and an understanding that situates Christians in relation to the emerging world around them, we can locate the theological thought of Jürgen Moltmann. His was an even more anguished concern with a discourse on God that could address human suffering. This concern developed for him, as he recounts it, while he was in a prisoner of war camp, as he witnessed the dissolution of European society. Subsequently, he witnessed the global suffering inflicted by discrimination, persecution, and war and the many forms in which suffering continued to be built into ambitious human enterprise in the period after World War II. Reflecting on the mystery of Christ and of the Trinity, he formulated, in a number of published works, a theological discourse on God that offers amid suffering the foundations for a reconstruction of human community and a global society that evolves from the inspiration, the breathing in, of God's revealed and loving presence.

While in his Christology Moltmann thought much about the relationship between Father and Son that could allow for the Son's abandonment on the cross, in his explicit treatment of the Trinity he related the mystery of the three as self-gift and communion of love to humanity's efforts to build a just social reality. In exploring the mystery of the Trinity, he attends to history and to the eschatological pull of a kingdom whose blessings draw us into the mystery of the Trinity.[6]

For Moltmann, creation and redemption have to be present in considerations of the Trinity as this mystery is revealed to us. They are inherent to the mutual relations of Father and Son, supported by the love of the Spirit. It is in the pure self-gift of the Father to the Son and in the obedience of the Son to the Father in the response of self-gift, that we can

---

[6] See in particular Jürgen Moltmann, *The Trinity and the Kingdom* (San Francisco: Harper & Row, 1981).

grasp the meaning of creation and redemption as divine self-gift coming from within the mutual relation of the three. Even the "abandonment" of the Son to the work of creation and to the cross, and the Son's leaving the Father to take on this work, is inherent to an understanding of the divine mystery of triune communion.

On this basis, Moltmann offered what he called a "social model" of the Trinity, by which he meant that the divine communion serves as a model for relations in human societies. The relationships of Father, Son, and Spirit are open to the participation of men and women. Thinking of the mystery of the Trinity as one into which humans are drawn provides a pattern for interaction among them in the building of a just world and in preserving the work of creation. It is only in a freedom from self-centredness, in a freedom in giving of the self to others, and in a freedom from slavery to false ideals of human sovereignty, that human society may participate in the mutuality of the triune God.

Alongside Moltmann, or perhaps even before him, we need to put the work of Dorothee Soelle.[7] She too witnessed the disasters of war and persecution and the horror of the concentrations camps. Her inherited and well-articulated Lutheran faith seemed to crumble in the face of this, and she realized that churches needed to hear anew the Word of God in the midst of the destruction of a civilization. Though in her political theology there is not a full-blown theology of Trinity for the overcoming of death, it is there in seed. Her perspective is expressed in the hope that the revelation given in Jesus Christ can break open and transform the social structures of the world, inviting people to an exodus from familiar and institutional structures of authority and divine representation, in order to transform the life of those who suffer neglect, poverty, persecution, and oppression. In this process they change social and religious orderings. This is what she calls the political hermeneutic for reading Scriptures and doing theology. At the heart of this lies the truth of Christ as representative, first of humanity in its suffering and then of God.

As Soelle saw it, through the sinful actions of our race, God had withdrawn or was absent. This is because a representation of the divine could no longer be found in the established forms of politics, philosophies, theologies, and religious institutions. With their incapacity to respond to evil

---

[7] Dorothee Soelle, *Christ the Representative: An Essay in Theology after the "Death of God"* (Philadelphia: Fortress Press, 1967), 130–52. On her political hermeneutic see *Political Theology* (Philadelphia: Fortress Press, 1974), 55–69.

and to transform order into just order, these could not claim to represent God or to bring God into the world. Those who turn to the Scriptures to listen attentively to the preaching and the story of the death of Jesus find in him one who represents humanity in its suffering members. This is to represent the whole of sinful humanity by identifying with those who are in one way or another victims, who have no place and no voice in human affairs. His death is the utmost expression of this solidarity, but its sense is grasped in hearing his Gospel and in heeding his testimony before the political and religious powers of the world.

It is in this representation of humanity, and on the condition of this representation, that Christ is the representation of God. He gives an absent God, a God who has withdrawn, a presence and a name in the community of the Beatitudes. All the names that Jesus gives to God—whether Lord, God, Father—refer to the presence wherein he represents himself among the poor and the meek, the persecuted and the peacemakers. This is the way in which the Christ represented God in his own time and the way in which he represents God now through his disciples. He himself risks being misrepresented, being falsely represented through political or religious entities that lay claim to his authority and so, in turn, being made absent. His disciples who follow his way, who know the solidarity that he showed, can keep true representation alive by their faith, by their actions, by their testimony, and by their way of being community. Soelle does not at this point develop a theology of the Spirit, but what can be said following her logic is that the Spirit enables this, and the discernment of the Spirit is to be done as we see a presence of Christ in his disciples among victims and peacemakers, a presence that offers a breakthrough and a power to transform the structures of human community.

Hans Urs Von Balthasar

In a kind of dialectic with Rahner we have to consider the tremendous impact of the theology of Hans Urs von Balthasar.[8] The latter took pains to distance himself from Rahner, whom he thought too infected by an approach "from below" and so from a theology of God which grounded an understanding of the divine and of revelation far too much in an understanding of the human. Von Balthasar's insistence was that

---

[8] A small but significant early work of von Balthasar is *Love Alone Is Credible* (San Francisco: Ignatius Press, 2005).

a true understanding of the analogy of being, or of humanity's participation in the divine as the very core of human being, has to start with
what is given in the descent from above, in the gift coming from God, in
the revelation given by God. The only thing that counts for the norm of
beauty is the cross of Christ, his self-emptying and his descent among
the dead. The symbolic manifestation whereby God reveals himself
shows the extent to which the Son, in the power of the Spirit, entered
into the suffering and even the death of humans distanced by sin from
God. Only by responding in faith to this revelation do humans recover
the image in which they were created and take their part with Christ in
the drama of the conflict between the generous divine freedom shown in
Christ and the parody of freedom displayed in those who pursue their
own interests and autonomy of being and action.

Von Balthasar centred his theology of God in the cross of Christ.
Even though he does not spell out the social implications of the *kenosis*
of incarnation and crucifixion, his formulation of the tension between the
divine freedom that is given expression in Christ's *kenosis* on one hand
and the hubris of human freedom on the other provides clues for the
formulation of a social ethic. Here, the manifestation/realization of the
reign of God is to be understood in terms of the human freedom taken
up in the Word Incarnate and exercised as *kenosis*, the self-emptying in
agape which is a participation in the divine *agape*. This tension between
two freedoms was lived out by Christ even to the descent into hell. It is
a tension, a witness to the kingdom, by which his followers in turn and
in the power of the Spirit may live as this struggle continues. It is this
consideration of freedom that is replete with untapped reserves for the
formulation of an ethic of justice rooted in the Divine Trinity.

The image of the self-emptying God in Christ who is without power
and dominion, the kenotic Christ whose kingship is discerned in service
and slavery, is the centrepiece of understanding the incarnation. Since
the slave/servant is the very presence of God amid prevailing political
and ecclesiastical orders with their hierarchies, an ethic of divine descent
puts a bold question mark in the face of political and ecclesiastical orders
patterned on domination and submission. Precise prescriptions, firm
commands, clear directives, and order—these are not the most fitting
expressions of this ethic. It is not conveyed principally through ethical
teaching but through ethical example. It stands forth in the witness of the
children of God who testify to the cross and to its promise of freedom.
It is in their testimony that the *kenosis* of God shines forth in weakness

and vulnerability. This summons us to an *agape* which comes to full form in a reconfiguration of justice as it is commonly understood into a love that moves us toward the transcendent, a transcendent which is itself to be known in the striving of a people who live by hope amid oppression, suffering, and despair.

Feminist Theologies of Trinity[9]

Turning to the contribution of feminist theologies, many names come spontaneously to mind. Here, we will rely extensively on the overview provided by Elizabeth Johnson. When we consider injustice we find that its name is gender-tinged. In many societies and in the church itself women have been made inferior, marginalized, and even excluded. They have not had the same freedom of activity as men, they have been kept outside systems of administration, and symbolic constructs have not been comprehensive enough to give proper recognition of their particular life force. In developing feminist theologies of the Trinity, a full-blown grasp of God's active *agape* comes into play, a love that is divinely originating self-giving and life-giving energy. Divine love and action are not simply concepts. They denote the divine at work in creation. Images drawn on the experience of women are needed to properly speak of the love of God and God's love alive in ecclesial and human communities. A theology of Christ also has to build on feminine associations, and speaking of him as God's Word has to be complemented by speaking of Divine Wisdom. In a relational framing of the incarnation we know that it is impossible to speak this Word and Wisdom without finding it in the mouth of Mary when she speaks prophetically, as in the song we call the *Magnificat*, in the testimony of the women to the risen Christ, or in the gifts of prophecy distributed to women and men alike in the time after the resurrection. It is singularly appropriate to speak of Jesus Christ himself as *Sophia*, God's wisdom, depicted as womanly in sapiential literature.

Feminist theology is of its nature critical of patriarchy in its many forms, but as feminist writing on God takes shape, writers find feminist ways of speaking of Son and Spirit, and indeed of the Father, so that the poetic and symbolic expressions of the Trinity may include women

---

[9] For a very helpful and creative overview, suffice to refer to chapter 5, "God Acting Womanish," in Elizabeth Johnson, *Quest for the Living God: Mapping Frontiers in the Theology of God* (New York: Continuum, 2007).

and men and their interaction in a more complete portrayal. This is vital too to the quest for justice, since the role of women in this enterprise is now to be acknowledged not only for its own sake but as increasingly important in building up local and world communities and societies. Unless the expression of revelation includes women in the vitality of the world and in the vitality of the church, its contribution to justice and peace remains truncated.

In taking account of the action of Christ and Spirit, the masculine images need the feminine. Indeed, feminist writers will contend that taking feminine images alone would give as complete a picture of the divine as taking masculine images alone. Too often only the latter have served, and it is this which gives rise to the critique of patriarchy. Johnson points out that a cluster of female images for the divine centres on women's experience of mothering.[10] Such metaphors are found, for example, in Isaiah 49:15 and Matthew 23:37. God's care for the world and divine care for the chosen cannot be rendered properly without recourse to the signs of motherly care. Maternal love means giving birth, nurturing the life of offspring to full flourishing, and defending children against onslaught. Drawing on such experience to portray God at work is inherent to an active sense of seeking justice, of turning to God's power at work in the world for the sake of those who suffer oppression and seek freedom.

Latin American Quest for God's Justice

Latin American theologians have been particularly sensitive to how belief in the triune God is inherent to the actions of their peoples who seek in faith and hope to transform the world. They connect this with the proclamation of the reign of God in the Gospel as found in the teaching and works of Jesus and with the story of the liberation of the peoples of Israel from their captivity in Egypt.

Leonardo Boff is among writers who, in some resemblance to Moltmann, look for a social model in the loving communion of the Three. Boff draws on the mystery of the Trinity to develop the understanding of community which is needed to enliven the social realm and to give true freedom to its citizens.[11] What is particular about Boff as complementary to Moltmann is his place in liberation theology, his concern with the

---

[10] Ibid., 100.
[11] See Leonardo Boff, *Trinity and Society* (Maryknoll, NY: Orbis, 1988).

world of the poor and the injustices which they suffer, even as they look to the Son and to the Spirit in hope for the eschatological fulfilment of the blessings of the kingdom. Through his encounter with Latin Americans, Moltmann himself extended his thought on God's presence to creation beyond the European situation so as to include the sufferings of peoples everywhere as well as the devastation of the environment caused by the ambition of human pursuits.

Jon Sobrino's theology of the Trinity[12] is more directly related to the experience of God in the activities which lead to social change, though he does not follow a social model of divine relations. He places the accent of his Christology on the resurrection of the Crucified One. Therein is found the seed of a theology of the Trinity, known in liberative action. In the resurrection of Jesus of Nazareth who was crucified for his claimed relation to God-Father in the midst of his mission among the poor, Sobrino finds a symbol of the fulfilment of a concrete life of mercy and compassion which is expressive of solidarity with the poor and of serving the reign of God in their midst. The church which lives by the Spirit of Christ is the church among the poor and the church living for the poor. The trinitarian reality of God is discernible in those who follow Jesus in the making of history in service of the kingdom, for there too the Spirit is at work and the true divinity of God is made known in the revelation of the Father through the lived practice of the Beatitudes.

It is in relationship to the historical reality of Jesus as God's Son, in his mission, his crucifixion, and his resurrection, that the presence of the Spirit is known; it is also in this way that God makes the divine self known as Father. This is to say that the revelation of both Spirit and Father is to be found in Christ. The Spirit is alive in the midst of oppressed peoples, appearing in their hopes, their fears, and their activities related to transforming the world. It is present in those who live a solidarity with the poor in the practice of the Beatitudes and in the hope symbolized in the resurrection of the Son. In this following of Jesus in the power of the Spirit, we come to know what it means that God is Father. This address (God to us, we to God) shows how God, who is origin and destiny of all created reality, is provident in history in the demand of the oppressed for the justice which gives true freedom.

---

[12] Reference is made here particularly to two of his books: Jon Sobrino, *The True Church and the Poor Church* (Maryknoll, NY: Orbis Books, 1984); *Jesus in Latin America* (Maryknoll, NY: Orbis Books, 1987).

Yet he is eschatologically present as beyond history as the one in whose loving care the fulfilment of hopes and freedom is yet to come and is indeed beyond earthly realization.

African Trinity

Since present concerns for justice are global, and since a just and peaceful global community is an eschatological hope, theology cannot afford to remain Eurocentric. However inadequate, some account is therefore given here of pertinent approaches to justice on the African continent.

When one asks how African theology thinks about struggles against poverty and oppression, it is the names of three theologians from the Cameroun that come most readily to mind, namely, Jean-Marc Ela, Meinrad Hebga, Engelbert Mveng. African theology such as theirs is very biblical in the sense that it shows a deep appreciation of story and of how God's story on this earth is mingled with the stories of peoples. While the Old Testament is about the story of Israel, God's immersion in that story makes Africans ask what God has to do with the stories (quite varied in nature) told by African peoples. Following closely the Synoptic Gospels, when the gospel is read as the story of how Jesus Christ preached and testified to the advent of the kingdom of God, it is asked how this story fits into African story, how it can be about the kingdom of God among all the oppressed of the earth and in particular of African peoples. In doing theology of this sort there is no doubt a great concern with suffering and evil, with all that contaminates and corrupts the development of human life.

The meeting point between Christ and African peoples in theologies that seek political and cultural liberation is that both Christianity and African traditional religion are religions of salvation. For Africans, salvation is not for the future but is to be experienced as present, as communal, and as affecting the totality of human and cosmic reality. Nature, persons, ancestors, and the unseen are bound together in cosmic oneness. There can be no well-being unless one is in harmony with one's community and with the cosmic totality. Social justice has to be conceived as vital to life in its entirety, along with the need for health, solidarity in building a common future, the overcoming of suffering, the passage through death to fullness of being. Some African writers say that life is mystical, precisely because it has to do with this earthly and cosmic balance. Where it has been disturbed, salvation is to restore it. When life is seen as a process of continual initiation into the fullness of life, there is a ready response to the story of the Pasch of Christ, which may be read from the vantage point of Hebrews 2:10, presenting Christ as the guide toward human perfection and salvation. When Christology is based on a sense of community, of Christ with his sisters and brothers, there is concordance between faith in Christ and belief in the church as a community of initiation into mystery.

The liberationist approach and efforts at inculturation present in African theology are not opposed or even separate. Some speak readily of what Africans suffer as anthropological poverty, having to do with privation of life's necessities, of any particular story, of cultural heritage. None can be recovered and restored without the others. The Christ who sets free has to be one who fits with a people's way of seeing life, nature, communality, and relations to God. For this reason African theology is not to be reduced to something homogeneous but is as varied as Africa's peoples and their cultures. There is most often a focus on the earthly Jesus and his commitment to the cause of the oppressed as the cause of God, but he is also seen as the one who brings people into touch with the divine. As the quest for justice and reconciliation is woven into African theology, social struggle is adopted as a heuristic tool in interpreting both the Gospel and the social situation. When the connection between faith in Christ and the reality of the church is made, theology is avowedly a community-based approach which, while reflecting on Christ, does so in reflecting on the community's actual experience of Christ. Images and titles given to Jesus Christ are taken from or resonate with African religious constructs. They have to fit with their experience and perception of the universe.

The Lutheran theologian, Kä Mana[13] has links with the Democratic Republic of Congo, Cameroun, and Benin. He offers a theology of God three-in-one which he relates to the foundational role of developing authentic consciousness in achieving inner personal and true cultural freedom. This is a genuinely culturally rooted theology and one which shows how, in Word and Spirit, African peoples may be freed from the dictatorship of filling the belly, alienation, and powerlessness which

---

[13] Kä Mana writes in French. English-speaking readers can consult Kä Mana, *Christians and the Churches of Africa: Salvation in Christ and Building a New African Society* (Maryknoll, NY: Orbis Books, 2004).

impedes development. Following the maxim that the Gospel has to take
root in cultures and not supplant them, Kä Mana writes of how cultural
resources serve both to bring consciousness to expression and to provide
the seedbed for reception of the presence of Christ and Spirit in African
peoples. It is by their promptings that they bring a new society into being
for the good of peoples suffering the anthropological poverty brought
about through the threefold dictatorship named above.

To do this he relates three sets of myths known to Africans to the
revelation of the God three-in-one as the God of love to whom Christ
gives witness in all his works and words and in his self-emptying on the
cross. These are myths about society and the relations within it which
can break it or make it, about the separation between God and humankind which grounds a loss of the basic values of human being unless it is
bridged, about creation and the formation of human life within it. Christ
has shown that suffering for others is the principle of new life so that
death, or the empty tomb, is not the end of life. He shows that there is but
one Father for all, beyond the ethnocentricity and scapegoating which
can be used to overcome alienation. He shows that humanity grows in
harmony with creation and is not rendered helpless by forces in nature
alien to humankind; in creation the true force of growth is the presence
of God three-in-one, in all of creation and in human consciousness. In
revealing the triune God, Christ offers an ethic of creation built on love,
on which a just and free society may be built. Kä Mana's position may
be summarized in this way:

> Christ places Africans and their evangelisers under the same universal
> obligation: that of building a world based on solidarity whose founda-
> tional myths would not be limited to their respective cultures, but be
> deeply transformed by being plunged once more into the Spirit of God
> the Father and Creator God of love, with the intention of making all of
> humankind the sphere of his love and shared happiness.[14]

The expression of faith in God when God is called Father is relational
and, as far as God's presence in the universe is concerned, it is to God-
three-in-one. The relationship to God is formulated most appropriately
in story form, narrating in lived reality the relation of Christ to God,
even as this is thought of in terms of his relation with a people. Since
Africans think of the person as a being in relationship, and of growth as

---

[14] Ibid., 55.

a harmonious initiation into relationships, the relational view of Christ fits into a vision of the universe and of humanity's being in it. For an African vision of Christ, it is appropriate to quote a paragraph from one theologian, F. Eboussi Boulaga, in which he contrasts a typical hero myth with the story of Jesus Christ:

> The hero is not a god. Jesus Christ is not simply God and nothing more. He is the child of the Mother, the Son of man, before he is the Son of the Father or Son of God. He is the figure of fulfilled humanity for us. . . . Jesus is not everything. He is not the Father. His glory, his definitive being are received by him from the Father, in an everlasting being-together with the Father. The communion of Father and Son has not yet appeared. Christ in glory is yet to come, at the consummation of the ages, according to the faith that is hope.[15]

With this perception of Jesus Christ, Boulaga joins our communion with him through the gift of the Spirit: "But humanity is fulfiled only in identifying with the life of the Spirit animating the community, for the Spirit is life."

A strong feminist note to this eschatological hope is added by some African women theologians. This is important on a continent where some societies remain strongly patriarchal and where women suffer much abuse, so that their position in undertakings for the future needs to change. An example that serves us here is that of Mercy Amba Oduyoye in an article written for the circle of concerned African women theologians.[16] Like other women writers, she writes from her own context and subscribes to a particularly African perception of reality as a world in which there is no sharp dichotomy between the physical and the spiritual, so that the same patterns run through all things on earth and in the heavens, welding them into a unified cosmic system. Nevertheless, she adduces a distinctively feminine way of seeing and living this reality. In presenting the mystery of the God revealed through the Word/ Wisdom and Spirit at work in the cosmic system, women bring their own experience and insights. Important to them is the study of God's

---

[15] F. Eboussi Boulaga, *Christianity without Fetishes: An African Critique and Recapture of Christianity* (Maryknoll, NY: Orbis, 1984), 144.

[16] Mercy Amba Oduyoye, "The African Experience of God through the Eyes of an Akan Woman," *Cross Currents* 47, no. 4 (1997–98): accessed at http://www.crosscurrents. org/african.htm.

hospitality in the forms of African hospitality and the location of women in the household, in light of the vision of God as the Great Householder who empowers all and recognizes all as children in a parent's home and around the one table. In face of what they have to suffer, women experience God as one who sustains them in times of dire need and who brings victory where it is least expected. They express their experience of God in affirming cultural beliefs and practices while they feel called by God to denounce and to deconstruct oppressive ones.

The position of African theologies may be summarized by noting that, given the concern with relations, the Christian traditions about the Holy Spirit find a ready place in Christology, ecclesiology, and a theology of hope. Being the gift of God's own life, the role of the Spirit is to promote the initiation process which is vital to participation in much of African community life and to enliven and heal relationships for the good of the community, society, and the universe. To call the Spirit the eschatological Spirit, and to see the pentecostal pouring out after the Pasch of Christ as eschatological realization, fits with the African need for an immediacy of salvation. It is said that, in general, African religions had no myths of the end time, no concept of history moving forward to a future climax, but they were always about serving present relationships. When suffering, natural or human imposed, came their way, people thought of God as having withdrawn and, if ready to speak, to do so only through mediators. Encounter with the Gospel has given African peoples, and even a viable community of peoples and nations, a concrete eschatological hope and a goal for human life that transcends the broken order of things as calamitously experienced at the present moment of African history.

Asian Theologies

While Asian theology is often difficult for people in the West to grasp, it may be the most challenging of all in the present global situation, where ecological abuse and human poverty are intertwined in creating suffering and exploitation. A trinitarian theology written from an Asian perspective requires a change of perspective, a vision that gets beyond all dualisms in the way in which the human, the cosmic, and the divine are seen as one. By the conscious interiorization of the mystery of the Trinity, human persons are inserted within a mystery which is "cosmotheandric," where God is seen as mystery within the reality of the cosmos. Humans are within this mystery.

This Asian theology develops in a context of interreligious dialogue and in a much different cultural context from ours. In this situation, wherein Jesus is the "today" of the poor as seen in the work of the Indian theologian Felix Wilfred, some theologies of the Trinity attend to two things that are vital to the promotion of justice among Asia's peoples. These are the call to accept suffering and at the same time to find ways of rising above suffering without negating its necessity. Such insight arises from its role in Asian religions and philosophies. It is therefore pertinent for Christian theology to learn how to talk of suffering. The key to this is to relate the reality of suffering and the redemption from suffering to God through Christ, God's Son, who became a willing and obedient victim for the sake of others.

Something else to be noted is the importance of harmony in Asian religions and philosophies. This means that Asian cultures and religions offer Christians key ways of speaking of harmony, of a harmony that is necessary for justice among mortals and for peace with the environment, seeing this as a harmony that originates within the divine communion of Father, Son, and Spirit.

In this communion enfleshed in Christ we see the unity of the human beyond the dualism of matter and spirit as well as the unity of the divine. When Jesus says, "The Father and I are one" (John 10:30), he speaks beyond the kind of speech and action which separate the divine, the human, and the material. In this pronouncement we also hear how there is no dualism between being Word and being Son: the two namings are expressive of communion between Jesus and the Father. If in John's gospel, for example, the name of the Word has priority in some passages, this only emphasizes that salvation as creation includes the entire universe of God's creation. Jesus speaks out of his sense of communion with the Father who is source and destiny of all things, creator of a world in which the dualism between human and earth has to be overcome.

Within this vision of reality there is also an understanding of what constitutes sin. It is to place oneself (individual or corporate being such as people, race, gender) outside this communion, this oneness beyond dualities. It is to live from opposing dualities instead of within the mystery where all are one. Crises in economics, in politics, in the ecosystem result from living in opposition or separation instead of from a conscious vision of oneness. If this is restored in Christ and in communion with Christ in the Spirit, there is new possibility of just action. Reconciliation is more than ceding something to the other or living in a way of trying to be and act together. It is to let unity be restored as Christ shows us it may be. To work for the now as the "today" of the poor is to be aware of those who suffer most from lived dualities. It is to know and act as though there will be no justice without a reconciliation that mirrors "cosmotheandric" communion, and there is no human reconciliation which is not a reconciliation with earth and cosmic reality.

One particular example will serve to illustrate how interreligious dialogue on the concerns of peace and justice brings Asian theology back to a fresh reading of the Scriptures as primary theological source. An author who is much concerned with justice and who writes theology from within the practice of dialogue between Christianity and Buddhism is Aloysius Pieris[17] of Sri Lanka. In reflecting on Jesus in light of the Buddha, he opts for a double *ascesis* as the nucleus of an Asian theology of liberation. The first is the struggle to be poor, the renunciation of biological, emotional, and physical ties that bind to particularities and blind to the extent of communion with others and to the depths of being. This makes possible a deeper communion with others and with creation and, more fundamentally, with the Spirit who is at work in the human story and in human lives, as in the story of creation.

The second *ascesis* is what he calls, using biblical terms, the "denunciation of mammon," the self-interest "which organizes itself into principalities and powers." He is writing here of forces and systems that benefit either the self or particular interests, even of particular countries, to the detriment of others and to the squandering of resources.

By this double *ascesis*, the struggle of Jesus for the poor unfolds as an "agapeic involvement" in the struggle against poverty. What is key to the role of Jesus in this struggle, and so to the role of his followers, is the total self-gift, the total personal disinterest, of *agape.* It is therefore in the story of Jesus and in the story of his followers that we see the presence of the Trinity in the kingdom of eschatological expectation. In Pieris' view, a theology of the Trinity, therefore, does well to pursue what is unfolded biblically by use of the terms *theos, logos,* and *pneuma. Theos* designates the one whom we invoke as source and summit of life, the beginning and the end point of human history, leading not to a cessation of conscious activity but to a consummation of collective history. This reality of *theos* is revealed to us and takes its place among us in the *logos,* in Jesus Christ

---

[17] Aloysius Pieris, *Love Meets Wisdom: A Christian Experience of Buddhism* (Maryknoll, NY: Orbis Books, 1988), esp. 129–35.

and in his proclamation, for he is the means of God's presence and the one without whom we do not have access to God and within whom we are one with the Father. The *pneuma*, active both in Jesus and in his followers, is God's activity from within, the personal and collective promptings to seek the good and to order all things in such a way that they are brought into a collective communion in diversity, a diversity which has its consummation in God/*theos* and which includes nature and cosmos as well as human mortals.

Theological Options of This Work

In all of the theologies surveyed in this chapter we see that access to the triune mystery of God is only through communion with Word and Spirit and that to heed these it is necessary to retrieve the biblical basis of revelation. We have learned from all these theologies and keep their concerns and orientations in mind. To respond to what is needed in writing of divine justice, however, in this work we show a preference for approaches influenced by Karl Barth in his insistence on the uniqueness of divine revelation which knows no true analogy and of Karl Rahner in his understanding of divine self-communication within human life and history. In working with the Trinity in terms of God's self-revelation and self-communication, respectively, Barth and Rahner both caution against the limitations of the word "person" in contemporary discourse about the Trinity because of the way in which it has been influenced by Enlightenment thought. The limits of the social model, for all its important and necessary insights, is that it appears to import a notion of human person into the trinitarian communion, going beyond what can be said of the work of Word and Spirit in the world. The focus that we give to the Trinity as foundation of justice is on *the mission of Word and Spirit* while we refrain from looking at the eternal communion of the three as a social model for human community.

This option puts a theology of divine justice in line with the thought of Augustine and Aquinas, not for the sake of the analogy used to describe the emanations within God, but because they invite us to look to the acts of mind and heart, of intelligence and love, wherein the gift and presence of the Word and Spirit are known as sent into the world by the Father. It is not a matter of using a grasp of Word, in insight and judgment, and a grasp of love as giving to find in these an analogy for conceiving the divine relations and persons. It is more a matter of finding in intuition of truth and good, in judgment of what is good and wise conduct, in loving even to folly, the presence and truth of divine self-communication. This is something which is read simultaneously in a prayerful study of the Scriptures, in the story and modes of divine salvation, and in the lives of those who live the imitation of Christ, Word and Son, and are open to the Spirit. In the acts of those who are discerned to possess divine wisdom and live by divinely inspired love, we are given a revelation of the mystery of God. When we find this in the service of the world, and not only in a sealed ecclesial community, we are given the inspiration of a divinely given justice in the service of humanity's full salvation from sin and evil.

Even as Augustine and Aquinas use their analogies to speak of eternal divine life, we cannot forget that they found these in a grace-filled world, in persons and communities whose action in truth and love was that of humans made resplendent in the flesh by being and acting in the image and likeness of God according to the mind of Christ. In this way we see at work in our midst the desire and work for the justice which is the life-fulfilling action of the Word and the Spirit sent into the world to abide in God's creation. Efforts to serve all peoples in their diversity and at the same time work toward a just and peaceful global community are testimony to the Word and Spirit that come from the Father.

We certainly do not wish to give a strictly individual sense to the workings of Word and Spirit. These do not show up simply in the heart of the individual person, as some might interpret Augustine's and Aquinas' analogies. They are present in communities and in intersubjective operations with cultural and linguistic rootings. They are not purely mental operations. They are embodied. Allied with a practiced openness to God, they reveal themselves in deed, in story, in poetry, in hymn, and in ritual. When John's gospel says the Word was made flesh or the Spirit blows where it will, the human, social, cultural, and religious aspects of this revelation are to be given their full measure in that more abundant life which, being divine, is fully human.

This analogy of Word and Spirit at work in the world, and in a particular way among Christian believers, cannot be recovered today without looking to the fact that in offering life from generation to generation, a fundamental locution is that of story. This is the foundation for all speculative thought, for all spiritualities, and for all institutional determinations "in time and place" of how a community of believers coheres and pursues a common vision and even a concrete enterprise. The recovery of the foundational role of story is very important at the present moment of the life of Christian communities. Metaphysical constructs which relied on concepts and paradigms of causal order are rightly called into question. So are institutional forms that rely heavily on quasi-historical notions of a divine institution that has given a once and for all constitutional form to office and code of life. Comparatively, when dogmatic formulations are considered in the settings in which they emerge, new efforts of interpretation are required. With all such necessary deconstruction of thought and institution, a return to founding stories is needed, as will be seen later when speaking of the naming of the God of justice. The work of the Word and Spirit can then be considered, starting with how their operation is found in stories which are always linked to a vision of reality and to an ethical way of life.

In one way or another, the role of story hovers in all the theologies of Trinity reviewed above. Even the trinitarian retrievals in face of rational thought or dogmatic stubbornness in Barth and Rahner are located within a story, the story of how the Enlightenment came about and the story of the retrieval of an active human subject who makes history. With Moltmann and Soelle, the relation to a very particular story, the story of suffering in our time, is much more explicit. As for von Balthasar, he prefers the category of drama but finds salvation as a drama in which God and humans are agents working toward a destiny whose apocalyptic close is written large in the final book of the Scriptures, an apocalypse in which the beginning of the drama in Genesis is echoed.

In Moltmann and von Balthasar, one suspects with their critics a temptation to collapse the variegated human/divine story into the inner story of Father and Son and their bonding in the Spirit. Looking to the workings of Word and Spirit from generation unto generation, from one particular setting to another, we work outside such an assumption while still looking at revelation and salvation as the working out in locution, symbolic action, spirituality, and ethic of a story. The story is that of the convergence of the actions and even suffering of Word and Spirit in the world with the story of the suffering and the actions of those persons and communities within which they work. As we will see in the chapter on naming, this makes this work to a great extent privy to those who question the existence or at least the rightness of a Grand Narrative into which all narratives are subsumed. The differentiation in the recovery of the story of Jesus, within the Scriptures themselves, and in the ways in which it is spoken and acted out among diverse peoples and in diverse epochs is a challenge. The challenge of this diversity is a challenge to a theology which is grounded in the confession of divine advent and promise and yet attempts to be the thinking out of justice, reconciliation, and peace for the many who remain many even when they seek to be and act as one community of conversation, suffering, and action across the globe.

This attention to the activity of Word and Spirit in humanity and in the universe opens the way to a diversity of theologies which are attentive to personal and community consciousness and its growth, and so also to the forms in which this consciousness is expressed in their cultural diversity. This reference to their multiform presences makes conversation across cultures and across the globe possible. We have seen how European theologians look at the ways in which peoples are conscious of suffering and search for ways to turn to God within the forms in which this consciousness is given expression. We have also seen how theologies emerging from Africa, Asia, and Latin America take into account that plural consciousness which is expressed in their traditional religious and oral forms. If we relate the gift of Word and Spirit to these peoples and churches, we can see how they find a home in the church and offer the possibilities of faith in the one God and of hope for the future of humankind.

Again, it is crucial to note that when pursing the foundations of justice in this plural conversation and interaction within peoples and between peoples, the main thing is to see God's self-communication in the gift of Word and of Spirit affecting personal life, affecting communities, affecting cultures, and affecting history. Indeed, this is the necessary premise to taking the inspiration from the analogies of Augustine and Aquinas when, and if, these are pursued. There is vibrancy to the act of speaking a word which cannot be lost. Speaker and spoken to, as well as milieu, are always at stake. While we may think of God's unique Word, when this is communicated to mortals it is necessarily couched in many words if it is not to lie dormant.

Already in the Scriptures, attending to the diversity of New Testament literature, we find the many ways in which Christ was spoken in order to be proclaimed and made known among different peoples and in different situations. There is a universal power of life in the action of love, and we are witnesses to the many ways in which the Spirit brings life, heals, raises up witnesses, acts for the whole through particular charisms, testifies to Christ in face of principalities and powers, and groans with creation. In working out the practical implications of this insight, however, in keeping with all that has been said about doing a theology for our contemporary situation, we wish to keep before us all that has emerged about hearing and seeing God in face of suffering in the theologies to which we have appealed.

With this accent on the Word made flesh and the Spirit in the world as the place where God is revealed in true justice, there is due place for the image of divine *kenosis*.[18] It is in the flesh of Christ that we see the self-emptying whereby divine truth and love are made known. The abasement of Jesus whereby he associated with the lowly and on the cross identified himself with the lowliest of the low is the way by which God makes divine presence known and by which believers have access to the Father. The identification which Jesus takes on through *kenosis* is an upheaval of oppressive social and religious orders which tend to place divinity among the powerful and within the exercise of their powers. It is a reversal of expectations of God, and one hopes for a reversal in human social and political life that may result from this new perspective on how God sees the world and on how God is in the world. By the work of the Spirit, the Son, and through the Son the Father, continues to be present in this way in the history of the church and in the history of the world. God presses against reality to make it known that truth and justice are among the weak of the earth and that this justice cries out for a way of being and acting which looks to the redemption of what is oppressive of both humans and nature.[19]

The question posed earlier is: Can faith in the presence of the triune God in the world and in the human story offer a vision of reality beyond the bounds of reason which can mediate between the immediate world of peoples and the greater community in which all participate? The urgency of this has come more into our vision as the link between human exploitation and the exploitation of nature's resources comes to light. This has also been the concern of Christians, especially of many working with indigenous communities. It is not surprising that Leonardo Boff completes his interest in serving the poor peoples of the Latin America with a work titled *Cry of the Earth, Cry of the Poor*.[20] At the conference

---

[18] See David N. Power, *Love without Calculation: A Reflection on Divine Kenosis* (New York: Crossroad, 2005), 38–60.

[19] On the Spirit and *kenosis* in the mission of the church, ibid., 67–74, 147–48.

[20] Leonardo Boff, *Cry of the Earth, Cry of the Poor* (Maryknoll, NY: Orbis Books, 1997).

of bishops of Latin America and the Caribbean (CELAM) at Aparecida (2007), the bishops pledged themselves to the service and preservation of local sustainable communities whose habitat and cultural perception of the world are disturbed by the ecological effects of industry and the use of natural resources, especially among indigenous peoples. In this there is at least an implicit recognition that it is necessary to present the Gospel in such a way as to complete and blend with indigenous people's cultural perceptions and cultural ways of living. In other words, there is to be a blend and mediation between the particular and the universal, between sustainable community and larger global community. This concurs with the analysis of social reality which was presented in chapter 1 through the eyes of Jürgen Habermas.

Conclusion

In the above we have tried to show how theologies of the Trinity have been related to a particular epoch in history, to the suffering and the thirst for justice of peoples enduring the pain of humanity's sin, both personal and social. When we looked at African theology we saw the interest in presenting Christ, God, and Spirit in such a way as to insert the Gospel into people's own religious and cultural perceptions while at the same time giving them a sense of belonging. This within a concourse of peoples brought together in the active love of the One God who so loved the world that he sent his Word and his Spirit to save it from sin and to mediate life. In Asian theology we noted the view of reconciliation inherent to justice and the retrieval of a deeper sensitivity to the communion between the divine, the human, and the cosmic. Feminist theologies from all continents remind us how truncated is the image of God and of divine activity in the world if presented in uniquely and even dominantly patriarchal terms. We cannot hope to mediate between the particular and the universal in people's lives unless we can speak of God in such a way as to express how this loving concern embraces both the particular and the universal.

Finally, we return to the citation of Richard Falk on the place of religion at the end of the previous chapter. Of theologies of the Trinity seen in this light we can say the following. First, those whom we have quoted find a fresh starting point in reading revelation in the suffering of many kinds to which humanity and earth are subjected today. Second, when attention to particularity is inherent to considerations of the Trinity at work in forging human community, this has popular roots in that it attends to the particular religious expression of the peoples who suffer. Third, the mission of Word and Spirit clearly invites an ethical commitment to solidarity. This is a solidarity of the entire human family in looking for a common earthly destiny and, most of all, a solidarity with those who are victims of injustice and discrimination. Fourth, since these theologies are concerned with divine self-communication, that is, the divine missions and divine presence in the world, they are clearly theologies grounded in a sense of transcendence that relates to human origins, to the origins of creation, and to the transcendental destiny in the heavens and the new earth promised in the resurrection of Christ and in the pouring out of the Spirit. Fifth, with an eye especially to the world of the poor and to their faith in the Gospel, faith in the triune God who is present in our midst is the ground of hope for the future of a beleaguered humanity and an exploited earth. Sixth, since there is response to excesses of Enlightenment and rationalistic thinking written into many of these theologies, they clearly express the conviction that hope in the transcendent entails a recognition of human limits and an openness to the gift of life that comes through God's triune self-communication. Seventh, there is a revival of what it means to be committed to the world while finding identity in the gift from God and in communion in the life of Word and Spirit. Eighth, in the understanding of the needs of the times and the mission of Word and Spirit set forth in these pages, it is clear that these theologies address the necessary place of reconciliation in the movement to a global human community of interaction and mutual respect. Finally, when the diversity in religious expression found especially in African, Asian, and Latin American peoples is integrated into the living of the Christian Gospel, peoples who have been exploited and reduced to cultural poverty can find their identity anew as communities whose sustainability is acknowledged as a necessary part of the planning of a global human community.

Suggested Readings

von Balthasar, Hans Urs. *Love Alone Is Credible*. San Francisco: Ignatius Press, 2005.
Though only recently translated into English, this is an early and quite short
work of the writer in which the perspectives and concerns of his theological
corpus are already set out.

Boff, Leonardo. *Holy Trinity, Perfect Community*. Maryknoll, NY: Orbis Books,
2000.
Boff makes the connection between Latin American liberation theology and the
mystery of the Trinity.

Ela, Jean-Marc. *My Faith as an African*. Maryknoll, NY: Orbis Books, 1998.
Translated from the French, this is an early and influential contribution to an
African theology concerned with what divine revelation says of liberation and
culture.

Johnson, Elizabeth. *Quest for the Living God: Mapping Frontiers in the Theology of
God*. New York: Continuum, 2007.
In this work, Johnson gives a very readable overview of some of the theologies
of God surveyed in the present work.

Moltmann, Jürgen. *The Trinity and the Kingdom*. Minneapolis: Fortress Press, 1993.
In this book Moltmann relates his theology of Time, Cross, and Church to
the mystery of the Trinity, with an emphasis on its social and transformative
implications.

Rahner, Karl. *The Trinity*. New York: Herder & Herder, 1970.
The short and influential book in which Rahner sets out his foundations for a
theology of the Trinity.

Soelle, Dorothee. *Essential Writings*. Selected and edited by Dianne Oliver. Maryknoll, NY: Orbis, 2006.
A very useful complement, treating of similar issues, to the work of Moltmann.

Thompson, John. *Modern Trinitarian Perspectives*. New York: Oxford University
Press, 1994.
A good overview of current trinitarian theology.

CHAPTER 3

Naming God as an Ethical Project

We follow up on the consideration of theologies treating the work of God through Word and Spirit and their contribution to a theology of justice by looking at ways in which God is named. Naming is in effect an ethical project, for it shows how faith in a God of justice is woven into the human story and how humans are to live in light of this naming. For Christians, God is always the Father of our Lord Jesus Christ, the one whose name we know from the coming, the ministry, the passion and death, and the raising up of Jesus as God's Son and Word. Even when we profess in the Creed that we believe in God the Father, creator of heaven and earth, we are speaking of the one named for us in the Christ event.

In this chapter we explore how relations and ethical projects are revealed and fostered through narrative and storytelling and other forms of speech. We call naming or storytelling itself an ethical project, for it is in narrative that reality is presented with its possibilities for the future. A few examples suggest how narrative fits into the intersubjective scope of living. First, for any communication between ourselves that goes beyond gentle nods, we need revealing stories and we need names. The woman, for example, who tells of her dying son may not have given her registered name, but in telling the story as one that had significance for the listener, she becomes "the woman who told the story of her dying son." To commit ourselves to aiding victims of natural disasters or of injustice, we are greatly prompted by hearing their stories. And we need stories cast in the form of opening up new possibilities.

The naming of God is always done in story, even when complemented by other forms of discourse. Since here we are looking for a trinitarian praxis of justice, we want to see how God's naming relates to this. This may seem difficult today when it is difficult to have an entire society subscribe to the same founding story or, indeed, for Christians to live with only one version of the Christ to whom they look for salvation. Instead of being a hindrance in authentic intersubjectivity, however, this is a fresh opening up of questions of justice pursued in Christ's name. We can look for possibilities offered today when some who are victims of oppression and discrimination cast the Christian remembrance in new moulds. The diversity of this remembrance exacts respect.

Introduction: God in Fragments

We are in a time when apparently solid constructions of truth do not stand firm, a time in which people continue their search for truth and justice in different places and in diverse ways. A common lament among the religiously minded is that what were once religious cultures have dissolved due to a gradual process of secularization. When Modernity or the Enlightenment is deemed the culprit, forms of thinking that are loosely called postmodern emerge. Outside the Eurozone, the effects of release from colonial domination lead people to revisit their own stories in the light of a newfound freedom and, if they are of Christian faith, to revisit the Gospel in the light of these new perspectives.

What we call the postliberal is one of these movements to reconsolidate faith.[1] The postliberal conviction of recent decades, with its distress over humanity's doings, is that the world has moved to the rhythm of the wrong narrative, or of one constructed from human ambition and human thinking that ignores God. What is needed, it is contended, is to offer an alternate narrative, one composed from biblical texts that, after all the work of biblical criticism and historical reconstruction, may be read with a *seconde naïveté* as the Word of God, a narrative of God's response to human sin and redemption, of divine rather than human justification. This is to be the foundation of preaching, of ethics, and of worship, so that the Christian community of believers might represent another way of being in the world through its faith in God's Word and its submission to Christ.

The reading of history in this form of the postmodern is that humanity, by reason of its rationalist turn and ambition, is left without a coherent sense of history, without a story by which or in which to live.

---

[1] A good example is Garrett Green, *Theology, Hermeneutics, and the Imagination. The Crisis of Interpretation at the End of Modernity* (Cambridge, UK: Cambridge University Press, 2000).

Christians themselves, in whatever efforts they make to renew their sense of mission, do not seem to imagine that tradition gives them a meaning in which they may immerse themselves, a tradition which they can pass on to others by word and ritual. The claim is that in the wake of biblical criticism, which opened strange questions about the historical Jesus in a surrender to Modernity, we need to return to the biblical story which, in its wholeness and pattern, has an inner and abiding coherence despite the many small stories that are interwoven and the diverse forms of discourse found in the Scriptures. It is on the basis of this story that Christians may offer a reconstruction of the world, a narrative of redemption and of hope that is God's own telling. Whatever needs reform in liturgy is to be done on the basis of this conviction. The incarnation of the Word in time gives us the capacity to read the signs of the times with his eyes and so to retrieve an eschatological perspective which is the fulfilment of all things in him. This reading of the incarnation tends to see it as a once and for all narration of an event which leaves its imprint on humanity and history. Consequently, the continuing possibility of manifestation in and through historical events, or a discernment through the Spirit, or a retelling of the story, takes a back seat.

Others who accept some conversation with Modernity, postmodernity, and a variety of cultures hold, nonetheless, to the idea of an enduring paradigm or grand narrative in the Pasch. In other words, whatever the differences, all can hear the same grand narrative; all find faith in God and in Christ through adherence to a life lived in the persuasion of this narrative. This risks overlooking any need for a consideration of new potentialities for narration or any need to look at how narrations can embody ideologies, as has been shown, for example, by feminist and postcolonial examinations of texts.

What is commonly lacking in these approaches is attention to the fragmented nature of the human story and to the fragmented character of the scriptural narrative or, in other words, to the diversity of narrative and of plotting events in time within a communion of faith. All might indeed hear a proclamation about life/death, about redemption through cross/resurrection, but they hear it in diverse ways that are not reducible to each other and in settings that are diversified through historical, social, cultural, being. The questions of justice that affect minorities and diverse peoples in a global age cannot be resolved in the name of God's action through Word and Spirit unless diversification, within continued conversation, becomes possible.

Even as the claim is made to capture a master narrative of the Christ event, it becomes evident that the acclaimed master narrative either does not exist, is fragmented, or is simply the bones of a plot in search of a story. To say, for example, that the master narrative of the Pasch is a constant is to pass over the fact that stories of the Pasch in Christian literature offer several diverse meanings for Christ's death and resurrection. There may be some plot lines or some claims to universal verifiability, but not a story or narrative. The four gospels themselves offer different takes on the mission, death, and resurrection of Christ, takes that may be compared but that are different in their retrieval of the story of Jesus of Nazareth, of the scriptural literature, of the meaning of Jesus declared Son of God to particular communities at specific times. This fragmented nature of revelation is still further manifest in Paul's writings as he brings the Gospel of Jesus Christ to non-Judaic peoples and offers fresh constructs of revealed truth, as in his adoption of images whereby to describe the lordship of Christ in Colossians 1:15-20. There is no possibility of giving a concordance that turns all this into one Master Story, but the tale of Jesus from birth to resurrection and glory has to be read in fragments, even as similarities are seen; the stories are put into conversation with each other, and the reference to the one person of Jesus of Nazareth is clear.

Frank Matera in his *New Testament Theology*[2] has done a careful study that shows the different trajectories followed in proclaiming Christ. In his final chapter he writes of one underlying narrative told from diverse starting points.[3] One might say, however, that what he offers as the underlying narrative is more a set of creedal affirmations than a story, creedal statements that offer a point of reference but that emerge in different sounding ways within the diverse narratives. A creed, like the early Apostles' Creed, serves as a kind of apostolic verification of fragmented narrating, but it does not supply for narrative as such. The plot takes on meaning for diverse communities only when it is the bones of developed narratives that can respond to the lived, the historical, and the cultural realities of different communities.

Again, as we have seen, in living and seeking justice in a globally connected world, both the universal and the particular have to be re-

---

[2] Frank Matera, *New Testament Theology: Exploring Diversity and Unity* (Louisville & London: Westminster John Knox Press, 2007).
[3] Ibid., 478–79.

spected. In light of this correlation, it is the nature of fragment, of a truth told in fragmented fashion, which is important to retrieve when we now consider the redemption offered in Christ to all peoples, and especially to the non-European world. European here is understood to include the North American Anglo-Saxon heritage that is itself now imploding with indigenous and immigrant populations. The Christ of history belongs to all peoples and their histories. It has to be woven into a narrative for each one that is for them a pattern of belief and of hope. As the proclamation of salvation was told in fragmented ways from the beginning as it was given to diverse peoples and communities, so it is to be told today in a poetics which draws together what has been heard, what is being lived, and what is hoped. As Paul Ricoeur puts it, the ultimate stage of *mimesis*, or effective storytelling, is the emplotment into a people's lifeworld which shows the potentialities of an action oriented to a possible future, a transfigured world of being.[4]

In a comparable if not identical way, with an eye on Asian reality and the proclamation of Christ in India, Felix Wilfred writes that in listening to and appropriating revelation, "the particular will be the point of reference and the universal will have a role of service to illuminate the particular."[5] The universal will then be not a constant or a *stasis* but the result of conversation and commerce between particulars or, as Wilfred puts it, the continuous process of overcoming the limitations of the particular. For this reason, in telling and shaping the story of Jesus, the fragmentary and the particular are not to be taken as the parts or particularizations of a given whole but "every partial and fragmentary and particular experience of Jesus and his interpretation is the point of reference, and each one of them can be corrected, modified, and expanded."[6] For the sake of universal communion, then, in faith and in the service of humanity, dialogue between the different becomes the means of overcoming limitations, of mutual understanding, and of empathy in knowing Jesus, as well as in serving the God whom he has revealed, and within communities continues to reveal, by the work of the Spirit.

---

[4] Paul Ricoeur, "Mimesis and Representation," in *A Ricoeur Reader: Reflection and Imagination*, ed. Mario J. Valdés (Toronto & Buffalo: University of Toronto Press, 1991), 137–55.

[5] Felix Wilfred, "Towards a Subaltern Hermeneutics: Beyond the Contemporary Polarities in the Interpretation of Religious Traditions," *Voices from the Third World* 19, no. 2 (1996): 128–48.

[6] Ibid.

Wilfred contends that mission often offered a presumed but disquieting universalism in the doctrine of God and of salvation as colonial powers conveyed the sense of a universal rule and civilization. While postcolonial peoples and communities free themselves from this, they are inevitably themselves quite fragmented economically, culturally, and religiously. One can note in passing that what Wilfred writes of Asia could in fact apply in a diagnosis of the situation in any place where, in the dissolution of the given, fragmentation results.

In the face of this, some Christian writers look for ways of preaching Christ that integrate these perspectives and values, placing Christ within the development of religious and cultural traditions, not in order to reinstate any past, but in order to offer a way of true development that belongs to different peoples in their own cultural diversity. Only by offering an integrated vision of life, not imposed from abroad but coming to life from within, can the more obvious needs of justice such as food supply, housing, and education be efficaciously addressed.

When the Gospel takes root anew in any cultural setting, the work of the imagination is needed to refresh the narrative. This is done when the work of Word and Spirit come together in the minds and hearts of a people. Even at times when it is not clear how the promised covenant fits into their lives, the Spirit working in the heart enables people to turn to God as Father, to place trust in Christ from whom nothing will separate them, to groan with creation, even as they are afflicted, suffer injustice, and are faced with trials and doubts about meaning. With the Spirit at work, the appropriation of the remembrance of Christ into their own story and their cultural expression is possible, thereby making it possible for them to see their lives afresh and to give living testimony to the Gospel and to the God who is present among them.

If Christ as God's Son or Word incarnate by the Spirit is to be proclaimed to peoples in their fragmented existence, this mission may well be served by learning from what was done in the fragmentation shown in narrating the Christ event to different communities in apostolic times. The principle is, in fact, offered in the Second Vatican Council's document on mission, *Ad Gentes*. It compares Christ taking a historical place among different peoples and cultures to the incarnation itself. This cannot be grasped as a historical reality unless located in the time and place of Jesus of Nazareth, in face of the political, economic, religious, and cultural factors of the world in which he lived. In writings about the beginnings of his ministry in Galilee, we see how fragmented the people's lives were.

This was by reason of political interference on the part of Rome and Herod, by reason of different rabbinical interpretations of the Torah, and by reason of the ill effects on land and water resources of agricultural policies not in accord with the Torah and its Jubilee prescriptions, which showed a primary concern for the needs of the poor and of the land itself. Besides seeing the testimony given to the advent of the kingdom of God as the time of salvation, one also has to see how the response to how Jesus reclaimed "what was said" in the Prophets and the Law offers the possibility of restoring a sense of order to the lives of those experiencing fragmentation.

One could say that this offers the bones of a narrative for peoples suffering poverty and want, peoples who do not have the chance to live fully integrated lives. To serve a global world order, it is necessary to have material privation in view and to foster economic, farming, and trade policies that offer a more just distribution of the world's resources. Nevertheless, if we speak of God who loves and who sent his Son and his Spirit, we are talking of a God who loves life in its fullness and in its integrity, as well as in its diversity. Aware of this we cannot but note how lives are broken in many ways, not just material. Cultures are shattered; relation to land and ancestors is disrespected; values are bent out of shape; the sense of a life extended beyond the present is made incompatible with the present; religious values do not endure. Life is broken into fragments and cries out for a word that restores its coherency. The Gospel of the kingdom of God has to speak to this need, but this cannot be done by harping on the urgency of restoring system and doctrine. Each people and each community has to be given the proclamation which enables it to find in its reception of the gospel narratives the seed of a complete and hopeful life, entering a global conversation with confidence and the sense of the possibilities offered.

Naming within Narratives

Searching out or composing meaningful stories has today become more important than ever. As is now commonly recognized, Christian faith is always rooted in narrative. Christianity over time obscured this by building a construct of doctrines and truths which it claimed derived from scriptural revelation. With recourse to philosophical traditions, it was able to put together a persuasive view of a coherent and hierarchically ordered universe in which God appeared as Supreme Being and

First Cause, giving being and provident movement to all of creation and particularly to human agents. In such a universe, religious and civic authorities were thought to hold their power from God and, in at least some sense, to rule in his name, or in the name of his Son, Jesus Christ. Unhappily, in its extreme forms, such a conception of the universe created obstacles to scientific research and exploration of the universe. It subjugated the majority of persons to the authority of others, inhibiting their free action and their power to shape their own lives. With the Enlightenment, its scientific research, and its philosophies of the human subject, this ordered vision could not hold sway, and the churches often resisted what they feared as the assaults of Modernity.

As Charles Taylor puts it, with the trembling of this edifice, the "social imaginary"—the accustomed way of imagining the social order—collapsed.[7] What replaced it was not another coherent vision of the whole but a secular story, that is, the story of human achievement in the construction of society and order with its own utopias. It is a common complaint that this story left too much to personal freedom and individual rights, that in its ambition it caused much harm to creation and to the poorer peoples and nations who seemed to be an obstruction to the great society envisaged. Whatever justice there may be to such a critique, it has become more apparent that religion has to appropriate positive insights into the human person, society, and justice that are found in this secular story. Rather than constructing anew the vision of an ordered chain of being, Christian writers find that placing Christian faith within its own story, and seeing how this converges with the secular story while instilling into it a transcendental thrust, is the path to travel. Within the telling of this story, the name of God emerges afresh as that of the one who enters the human story in events and in prophets, to give it true justice, true peace, and an eschatological orientation to what God still holds out for humanity and the universe. God is then named in story, not philosophically, though learning from philosophies Christians can better know the God who comes, the created universe, and the humanity for which God advents.

Among stories inherited, special attention is given to those considered foundational stories of the faith that is within us. Recall that the naming of God in biblical revelation and in Christian piety is always

---

[7] Charles Taylor, *Modern Social Imaginaries* (Durham & London: Duke University Press, 2004).

linked to story. By "piety" we mean the life of the inner spirit, its outer expressions, and the affective attachments that sustain it. As Paul Ricoeur puts it, "The naming of God is thus first of all a narrative naming. The theology of traditions names God in accord with a historical drama that recounts itself as a narrative of liberation."[8] The naming is connected most of all with the story of Exodus and the constitution of a people, then with the story of creation, and, of course most of all for Christians, with the story of Jesus of Nazareth, whom "you crucified and killed by the hands of those outside the law" but whom God raised up and freed from death (Acts 2:23-24). But there are also minor stories which give colour to the name, such as those of Esther and Job. And there are the prophetic utterances which cast light on the story of the people's captivity and return from exile. To know the name of God in his triune revelation we have to connect it with all these stories, as we also have to catch this name in the form of address when God speaks to us or when we presume to call him by the name as we have captured it in the response of faith. It is always a naming linked with experience in its most arduous and fearful, in its most hopeful and also in its mundane.

In short, the import of the Christ story is fully appreciated when it is heard in conjunction with three other kinds of story: creation story, covenant story, and morally orienting parable. These stories are separated into four genres but taken together their interpretation leads to the naming of God that takes place through and in them.

Certainly imaginative and mythical factors are employed in telling the Christ story. This is a crux for exegetes who want to sort out the exact elements of time and place when things occurred or who want to recapture the exact words of the Master. The relation to a historical figure, Jesus of Nazareth, whose place of death and burial is known and whose life and work were witnessed by the storytellers, however, remains always key to the significance of a divine event that belongs chronologically and geographically within time. When it is said that God is revealed as the Father of Jesus the Christ, this belongs clearly to a historical moment; it is a presence of God within human story.

The story, however, cannot be fully understood unless placed within a sequence of covenant stories that stretch back to Abraham. The making of covenant is a story of election, of God's free and loving choice of

---

[8] Paul Ricoeur, *Figuring the Sacred: Religion, Narrative, and Imagination*, ed. Mark I. Wallace, trans. David Pellauer (Minneapolis: Fortress Press, 1995), 225.

particular persons and of a particular people to be his witnesses among the peoples of the world. They are called to be the witnesses of a fundamental love of God that includes love of neighbour and love of the earth itself. The constant task of unfolding all that this story says emerges from reading the ethical part of the covenant remembrance and the subsequent story of Israel, which includes the story of the prophets of Israel, as they work out right relations with other peoples and persons.

Within this covenant time, creation stories are inserted to broaden their meaning. At the time of Abraham and the patriarchs and then of Moses, religious practice and worship had much to do with creating distinctions and divisions and even enmities among peoples. Creation stories, even when told as the story of beginnings, were limited in scope since often they had to do with the cosmos on view to a particular people, with their claim to place and land and so to their right to exist. The people of that eventual unity called Israel were similar to others in looking to a god to support their claims to land and the story of their origins, a story which is given the special form of promise and covenant. They move beyond a narrowed vision of ethnocentric cosmos, however, in reading the creation of the entire universe within their own story of divine covenant. A particular device for connecting the covenant with the people with creation is the placement of a covenant story in the protohistory of creation and of the beginnings of the human race. This is the story of the covenant with Noah and his family, who cannot be connected with any specific time and place. Its inclusion in the Hebrew Scriptures is a sign that the particular covenant that God makes with Israel embraces all of humanity and creation itself in its promises.

In interpretation, writers link the story of the beginnings in Genesis with the story of the endings in the book of Revelation, which is about the new heavens and the new earth of end time. That the formation of the canon put everything about divine revelation, about the revelation of God's name, between these two stories is significant. However particular events have to be in order to find their place within history, revelation is ultimately cosmic; it is about God's love for all creation and about the hoped-for fulfilment of the promise embedded in this love.

The ethical consequences of the story of Israel and of the Christ story come to the fore in the kind of story called "parable." This is a type of short fiction that uncovers a moral, provided it is properly related to the events of God's presence in Israel and then in Jesus Christ. It is a necessary kind of story if the ethical implications of the great story are to relate to daily life and practice. Elements of parable are found throughout the Scriptures. There is the example of Nathan's appeal to the conscience of David through the story of the pastor's beloved lamb torn from his bosom. There is the parable acted out by Ezekiel in breaching the fortifications of Jerusalem. The prominence of parable in the work of revelation, however, comes to the fore in the many parables attributed to Jesus in the gospels as he proclaims the advent of the reign of God.

Beyond this biblical naming, there is the ongoing story embedded in tradition. People across cultures capture the word they have heard and go through a process of naming which finds the God revealed, the God who acts, in their own stories or in the stories of their forebears whom they remember. That is why pieties and the living out of faith multiply, as it were, the forms of the one name as they continue to evoke the Father in the name of the Son and even venture a few names for the Spirit who animates them. When peoples as peoples face, or when church as church faces, into the future of a common life and a common hope, their remembering and their naming become practical and political in the sense that they cast the efforts to build a world of peace and justice in the form of a vision that inspires what is to be done, in honesty and truth. To quote Ricoeur again, the storytelling, the listening, and the naming "can nourish an ethical and political reflection inasmuch as they govern an anticipation of a liberated and revived humanity."[9]

In *God, Time, and Being,* [10] Ghislain Lafont writes of how we listen to and assimilate this naming of God in our contemporary cultural existence. With Enlightenment ideas prevailing, human societies may seem to get caught up in scientific knowledge and scientific development in a manner which seems to be "without exit" or without ulterior purpose. Consequently, postmodern critics ask what must die in established processes in order that lives undermined by such progress may blossom. The same critics, however, may say that the theology of God provides no answer, because divine belief also seems to have been imprisoned in closed systems of thought and action. In face of this, Christians have begun to admit that they have tried too hard to pin down beliefs and structures leaving biblical texts little room to breathe. In admitting the rightness of such criticisms of Modernity and of Christian expression,

[9] Ibid., 234.
[10] Ghislain Lafont, *God, Time, and Being* (Petersham, MA: St Bede's Publications, 1992).

Lafont invites us to turn anew to a hearing of the Scriptures, especially of its foundational narratives.

A founding narrative, such as that of Christ's Pasch or of the exodus covenant or of creation, is proclaimed and heard in ever-fresh ways to answer the need to discern divine realities in human and cosmic existence. God is always Other, one not imprisoned in human concepts or orders yet showing us his face. Every hearing of the Word or celebration of sacrament is an event of Other and a breaking out of the ordinary or the systemic. The language about God must respect this otherness.

The founding narrative of God's advent, in the very variety of its fragmented forms, is heard as a testimony to grace and to life from the One whose action is narrated. It is transmitted across time and cultures by and with the testimony of believers and messengers. But it is not about an event enfolded into linear time. It is about one that irrupts/interrupts time and the human modes of coping with time. It is "repeated," both in the sense that it is always to be given and heard anew and in the sense that, in being proclaimed, it is interpreted afresh in relation to particular persons, communities, and events. It is a naming that is counter to the expectations of myth, religion, and philosophy. This is because it is done through God's liberation of the oppressed, in his affirmation of the goodness of the world even in the face of sin, and in the death of Jesus on the cross, where, in his abandonment, God's fatherhood is shown in the raising from the dead and the conquest of death. This is far more than, and much different from, pouring out life to fill the void. When a community moved by Word and the Spirit grants it a hearing, the narrative grounds an ethic of existence, an existence which refuses to yield to death and sin and suffering, and testifies to the power of a liberating abundance of divine love.

For Justice's Sake: Naming within Suffering

Today, those of good will whose interest is the good of the human community, inclusive of all its members, are necessarily concerned with the suffering and the stories of the suffering. As we saw in citing Richard Falk in the previous chapters, one of the indicators of how persuasive a religion can be is how it embodies the reality of suffering. The extent of suffering has raised many questions about God. These take many forms: total rejection of such an idea; an agnosticism that allows people to focus on the human; a crisis of faith of believers; the enigma of the divine name for those who continue to profess themselves followers of Jesus Christ, imbued with the hopes raised by the story of his testimony in death and of his being released by the Father from the mouth of death.

To see how naming in face of suffering fits into the framework of story we can look to the fairly classical response given to the need for this naming by Benedict XVI in his encyclical on hope, *Spe Salvi* (35–40). At one point he enunciates a kind of general principle: "The Christian faith has shown us that truth, justice and love are not simply ideals, but enormously weighty realities. It has shown us that God—Truth and Love in person—desired to suffer for us and with us" (39). As to how this needs story to be persuasive, the encyclical offers us five indicators. First, there is the story of Jesus' own suffering and compassion as the revelation of a compassionate God in our midst. Second, there is in light of this a penetration to the depths of human being and action. Third, other stories of suffering within Christian history are evoked. Fourth, Benedict shows how in the story of the present, the end of time when love triumphs over sin and suffering is anticipated. Fifth, the story of the suffering of creation itself is included elsewhere in the corpus of his teachings in the story of salvation.

The encyclical refers to the story of the suffering of Jesus Christ, saying: "God cannot suffer, but he can *suffer with* humanity. Humankind is worth so much to God that he himself became man in order to *suffer with* humans in an utterly real way—in flesh and blood—as is revealed to us in the account of Jesus's Passion" (39). The remembrance of this suffering, God named as one who suffers in the passion narrative of Jesus, places even the sufferings of the present within the horizon of hope: "in all human suffering we are joined by one who experiences and carries that suffering *with* us; hence *con-solatio* is present in all suffering, the consolation of God's compassionate love—and so the star of hope rises" (39).

It is because of the perception of God in the person and story of Christ suffering with us that Benedict could say earlier in the letter: "the true measure of humanity is essentially determined in relationship to suffering and to the sufferer" (38) and that this holds true both for the individual and for society. Relation with another, and especially with another who suffers, is impossible unless all in a society are capable of compassion, of sharing the suffering, of suffering with the other from within the heart that wills the good. For this reason, Benedict contends that "even the 'yes' to love is a source of suffering, because love always requires expropriations of my 'I,' in which I allow myself to be pruned and wounded" (38).

In the course of the encyclical Benedict recalls stories from the church's lore as to how martyrs and others have shown how to live suffering in the light of hope. In particular he invokes the stories of martyrs: "we need witnesses—martyrs—who have given themselves totally, so as to show us the way—day after day. We need them if we are to prefer goodness to comfort, even in the little choices we face each day—knowing that this is how we live life to the full" (39). It is from them that we learn that "the capacity to suffer for the sake of the truth is the measure of humanity" (39).

Both the story of Jesus and the stories of others are placed within the light of the anticipation of the end. We are well aware that the eschatological imagination, as for example in the book of Revelation or the description in Matthew of the final judgment by the Son of Man, carries the story of suffering forward into the world to come, where it is evident both as something that endures in the Lamb and in the martyrs and as something that is overcome in the victory of the Lamb. To deal with this in a more conceptual way, at one stage in his encyclical Benedict attempts to retrieve the doctrine of purgatory and, incidentally, of hell in light of justice sought and injustice meted out: "Evildoers, in the end, do not sit at table at the eternal banquet beside their victims without distinction, as though nothing had happened" (*SpS* 44). What he is saying is that all human conduct, and specifically that of making others the victims of injustice, has to be seen in light of God's judgment on the world in Christ. We cannot look forward to an eternity in which the actions and sufferings of this world do not count. There is to be a certain heavenly redress, expressed here in the image of the banquet. While not discounting the possibility of hell, Benedict is intent on showing that the doctrine of purgatory requires an acknowledgment of fault and an act of purification in which it is Christ who is agent and where relations may be restored.

There is a risk in this of giving the impression that retribution and redress are put off until eternity, when things are evened out according to actions and situations lived out in human history. In other parts of the letter, however, Benedict makes it clear that divine justice and Christian action envisage an earthly justice which favours the poor and the oppressed victims of human ambition. We cannot properly conceive humanity, or recover the human story, unless we see that all are destined to eternal life. This is what gives persons their dignity even in the present.

In his recent messages for world peace, Benedict has pointed out that the fate of creation, however much we have to guess what it may be, is involved in this hope for the eternal. In some forms of piety and spirituality this is too readily offered as a consolation to those who suffer severe trials and even lack of hope on earth. It can lead some to a disinterest in the things of earth. This is, however, based on a false view of the hope of eternity, which rightly seen is tied up with how we respect the human person in the present and how we build societies and communities in the here and now that are, as it were, worthy of eternal life, expressive of the nature of life and love that is a presage of the eternal.

If we do not grasp that the suffering of Christ is compassion and solidarity and that in some sense God's suffering is his act of revealing, we do not know God's name. It is in the story of Christ, carried forward by the Scriptures into the eternal kingdom, that we see this compassion at work. At first it may seem odd, but one of the strong ways in which hope for the present is displayed is in the care taken with the burial of the dead and with keeping their memory alive, not just in monuments, but in tales told. One of the great catastrophes of natural disasters is that rites for the dead cannot be performed, and under oppressive regimes a great complaint is often made that the dead are deprived of the dignity of decent funeral rites. This is a tremendous assault on the human person and on the persuasion that living and dead remain bound together in communion and that the memory of the dead is to be kept alive. If the dead are not deemed worthy of proper burial, one may be sure that the living are not considered worth the effort of being assured justice and an appropriately human way of life. It is in the face of an end that we discover the importance of story. So what is done with the dead helps bring insight into the importance of remembrance in story, in a convergence of story, both Christ's and theirs. Put simply, if human life means anything, we must give proper burial to the dead and remember their story.

In terms of faith we can say that God loves the world so much that he assures it eternal life. We are invited to believe in a God who is named for the consolation of strength to struggle against evil and suffering for the betterment of earthly existence. Naming in face of suffering includes naming in face of the end, since the suffering of humanity and of earth seems so absolutely annihilating that it wipes out hope. That is why apocalypse is the end of the biblical story.

In Matthew 27:52-53 on the death of Jesus, signs are given that show that the time of the kingdom has come. Nature is perturbed, graves are opened, and the dead arise and even enter the cities. This is typical of how the end is anticipated as already present, even as the story continues. The Apocalypse, or book of Revelation as it is now more commonly called, narrates in imaginative fashion the end of history. With judgment, plagues, and other afflictions, all human constructions that are the work of human ambition and inflict suffering on others are wiped out. With the story of the triumph of the Lamb and of the heavenly worship, the narrative reaches its climax. There is much in this imaginary ending that resonates with people today, as we are faced with the end of civilization; the ending of cultures; the ending of peoples; the ending of languages; the end brought about by terrorist activity, global warming and climate change; and the pandemic of AIDS. Beyond these there seems no possibility of life. All this is named, as it were, in the Apocalypse. But the end is not the end. At the end of the stories of catastrophe there is the story of the triumph of the Lamb, he who is the Alpha and the Omega, the light that is never extinguished, the one who sits upon the throne and subjects all things to the Father. It is not an ending that humans can bring about, but a coming long promised. The story of apocalyptic destruction ends with the story of God's final victory. Whatever the chronology of composition, the Bible as we have it in hand begins with creation by God's word alone, with the Spirit of life hovering over the waters, and ends with the building of the heavenly city, and at the midpoint there is the incarnation of the Word to dwell among us.

We have to ask what kind of intermediate narrative embodies this sense of solidarity and hope. What narrative can be told that is faithful to the name of the God of those who suffer with hope in the face of the ending that God gives to the overarching story? We often feel compelled today to name martyrs and to name them in ways that relate to suffering for justice, for the building of authentic human communities and social orders. It is for this reason that the canonization of a person like Oscar Romero would be important. While the situation of early Christians was much different, we nonetheless find inspiration for ourselves in the way that the letters of Paul and the so-called First Letter of Peter speak of suffering.

Paul, even as he suffers persecution, shipwreck, incarceration, and bodily weaknesses, says repeatedly that nothing he suffers for preaching Christ can separate him from the love of God which is in Christ Jesus. The author of 1 Peter is addressing a community which is looked down on by others, apparently for religious and social reasons. He says to them, "Beloved, do not be surprised at the fiery ordeal that is taking place among you to test you, as though something strange were happening to you. But rejoice insofar as you are sharing Christ's sufferings, so that you may also be glad and shout for joy when his glory is revealed" (1 Pet 4:12-13). In other words, it is not despite suffering or outside of suffering that they know Christ, but, rather, they know him in the reality and in the story of their suffering by reason of the faith they profess. While the situation today amid global endeavours is much different, it is still true that God cannot be named in the revelation given to us unless it is heard and invoked in the midst of suffering and in the combat against the suffering of others. The great temptation of the household of the faith to which 1 Peter is addressed was to cede to the demands of the surrounding culture, to fit in with the way things were done, to yield to prevailing powers. Today believers can easily find ways of fitting in with a culture of self-interest or group-interest or seek the comfort of economic and social power in ways all too commonly in evidence. People can behave like this even in pursuing supposed spiritual ends, as when episcopal bodies camouflaged clerical abuse of children "for the good of the church." To act that way is not just a matter of disobeying God's law. It is to not know God, to not take the way which is the way of true wisdom and knowledge. Even as suffering is remembered and the story of the suffering told, God is named.

Narrative of a Covenant Made and Completed in Suffering

That the narrative about Israel has to do with a suffering people, and then about those who suffer among the people, is commonly recognized. God sends his servant Moses to lead the people of Israel to freedom, liberating them from the suffering of servitude to an unjust ruler. When the covenant is made, there are very special provisions about caring for the needy and suffering and the land itself. This is inseparable from the prescriptions about true worship. The rituals for Sabbath and Pasch are to keep the people mindful of their release as a people and of the suffering among them. These holy days and rituals cannot be kept unless the story is told and the youngest child keeps asking the question, "Why is this day different from any other day?" Later misfortunes of the people are often attributed to a failure to live by these covenant prescriptions, seeking instead a high place among the nations, with individuals and groups pursuing their own self-interest. It is not only the unjust among the people who endure war and exile, but these events themselves give birth to new poor of whom God nevertheless remains ever mindful. The story of Israel cannot be told without the story of the poor and of God's ever-repeated promise to which he binds himself by covenant.

We have already cautioned that the narrative of Jesus of Nazareth, the beloved Son of the Father on whom the Spirit descends, needs to be ever made concrete. His initial prophetic message about the kingdom is about being sent to the poor of his place and time, about breaking the chain of poverty even while expanding the horizon of all to a neighbourliness, a communion, with people of other tribes, peoples, and nations. His passion and death too are read as a testimony to the God of the covenant and of God's presence at this special hour in the face of the powers and authorities of time and place, religious and secular. His resurrection has meaning as God's testimony to him and as God's commitment to continue to be present among the chosen by the action of the Spirit, taking part in the ongoing struggle between life and death, suffering and wholeness.

A number of contemporary authors such as Ghislain Lafont and Gustavo Gutiérrez[11] have thought it wise to look to Wisdom literature for a keener insight into God's presence in Israel and in the mystery of Jesus. They do so by a reading of the story of Job in the context of our own time. This is done as an invitation into the mystical focus of the entire story of salvation, a focus which, even while prophetically committed to earth, arises to contemplation of God and to the desire for God even beyond the quest for justice on earth. Job is a sincere servant of the Lord and one who fulfils the law minutely, including the precepts about care of the poor and suffering. Yet he himself is cast into distress, want, and bodily sores. This gives him his own place among the poor and wretched. It is an invitation to a new solidarity, to cry out to God not simply on behalf of the poor but from their midst as one of them. His comforters cannot understand this. Their interpretation of the law and its just observance is that God rewards the good and confirms their bounteous lot. They do not question that the observance of the law requires looking after the needy. But they cannot understand why this just one could himself be reduced to this state. Inherent to the story is that in his experiences of suffering, Job has to find a new way of listening to the God of Wisdom and of praying, crying out to him.

---

[11] Gustavo Gutiérrez, *On Job: God-Talk and the Suffering of the Innocent* (Maryknoll, NY: Orbis Books, 1987).

The God of Wisdom who has created the earth and all it holds, who has chosen a particular people, is not confined within the earthly laws of wisdom. A perception of the ineffable mystery of God introduces the hearer and beholder to a fresh sense of how gratuitous is divine work and the gift of life. This is because it proceeds from the hands of a God who creates and saves out of sheer bounty and not of inner necessity. Such contemplation brings one beyond the immediate fulfilment of the covenant with the poor, beyond any immediate realization of liberation and justice, to an aspiration to that something greater. This is found only in a deepening communion with God. This leads to hoping beyond hope, to hoping for a kingdom that is beyond the kingdom of justice, which is to be sought now with an intense humility, self-emptying, and commitment, as exemplified in the story of the ultimately Just One, Jesus the Christ.

In listening to these narratives for an ethic, a way of behaving in the light of the story of God's self-communication, it becomes apparent that even the Decalogue as social code of spirit and action, or the evangelical ethic of the Beatitudes in the Sermon on the Mount and in the Sermon of the Plain, are to be interpreted within narrative. They inspire an ethical imagination within which rules may be set. When God is acclaimed as Saviour, the God of covenant, and indeed Creator, this affects the view of all reality and influences social mores. These Torah and gospel texts represent the vision of those who with trust and hope face the realities of inequality, repression, and discrimination surrounding them. They are inspired by a communal ethic, seeking to live together as one, giving witness as one to others. Heard and read under different circumstances, they invite readers and hearers to work out what we now call the "social doctrine" of the church, a way of thinking which is a guide and, in the midst of new realities and events, inspires the action that leads to the reconstruction of a more just world.

Naming for Creation

In his Canticle of Creatures, the lover of the poor and poor among the poor, Francis of Assisi, named creation for God and so God for creation. Humans and the creatures of earth and cosmos are in love within one another since they know they are all made by God and beloved of God. Together they can say a canticle of praise to God's name. Finding God reflected in earth, water, sun, moon, and even sister death, Francis could invite them all into a harmonious song of praise. Only sin could cut one off from this communion. What a curse that is.

Francis loved to sing the psalms with his brothers, and there he found the love of creation and the wonder at the Creator which fill the Scriptures. The development of the Hebrew Scriptures was such that they first recorded how the people knew God as the one who set them free from the slavery of Egypt and put nature itself at their service in their passage. In wishing to name creation in such a way as to give it one Creator and one creation story, the people of the covenant invoked the name of the God of the Covenant as God Creator. The two loves, of creation and of redemption, coincided.

With scientific discovery, the story of the cosmos and the stories of the human race blend. And so God is invoked as the one who is the origin and the life of the universe. With the knowledge that ecological disaster is upon us, those who know that there is no peace without justice and no justice without care for the environment search out stories and names that bring all into harmony, not by human effort alone, but in God's name. The Cry of the Earth and the Cry of the Poor sing in unison, and God is named in chorus.

The poor do not have to know the scientific paradigms that try to make sense out of the ways in which earth and humans belong within the same story. They know this ought to be so; they know from their own immediate environments that it must be restored and reconciled, and so their stories speak God's name. To account for creation, the respect owed it, and the place humans have in it, in the beginning they tell us there were many stories.[12] If the stories do not converge, if in the end they do not point to the one source and origin of all, there can only be warfare of one kind or another. Christians who have their belief in the one God, whom they name Creator and Saviour and, in the hope of God's justice, Father of the Lord Jesus Christ, own all these stories and piece them together like a quilt into their own. And so we have the God of one name, the God of no name and many names, the God who is Mamma Mercy and Lady Grace, and the God who gave up his Son to free the world from its mortality. And we have Jesus who is ancestor, elder brother, and even for prisoners "Bulldozer," for he has such power and force that he can free them.

---

[12] Agbonkhianmeghe E. Orobator, *Theology Brewed in an African Pot* (Maryknoll, NY: Orbis Books, 2009).

At root there is the fact that poverty has many faces and arises out of many stories. The suffering have many stories to account for the state in which they find the world yet still find it good. If Jesus and his Father and his Spirit are to be truly theirs, they have to relate to all these stories and all those who are storied, with perhaps the hope of one peaceful human family living in peace with the universe.

Redress: Feminist Naming

It is of interest to return to the classic work of Elisabeth Schüssler Fiorenza, *In Memory of Her*,[13] for the emancipatory power of a critical consideration of history and for the liberating power of history retold from the perspective of the disinherited and disaffected. Her approach to history is of interest not in a narrow feminist sense but in the broad sense that feminist theology reveals the social effects of all discrimination and ideology and offers a path of redress and retrieval for any who suffer under unjust structures.

The writer first draws our attention to the point that narrative or storytelling is always moved, if not always explicitly motivated, by some social interest in either stabilizing or critiquing the way things are. While we have, rightly it seems, talked much of the role of what the New Testament calls *agape* in naming God's work and presence in community and in the larger orders of things, *In Memory of Her* shows how even this concept could be woven into a story that fosters particular and even discriminatory interest. Looking to early community histories, the author writes of "Love Patriarchalism," an ironic way of showing that appeal to the distinctive characteristics of Christian love can be compromised by fitting it into the structures of patriarchy. It is thus that she dubs a way of retrieving and interpreting the Scriptures, especially the New Testament, which, in promoting the love that Christians are to have for one another, conveys the impression that they are to live peaceably within the prevailing social structures. Even within the church, they are to accept the roles and classifications assigned to gender and to particular groups of persons, such as slaves or servants, rulers and ruled.

As an alternate to this, Schüssler Fiorenza offers a way of reading the New Testament story of Jesus and his disciples which frees people

---

[13] Elisabeth Schüssler Fiorenza, *In Memory of Her: A Feminist Theological Reconstruction of Christian Origins* (New York: Crossroad, 1984).

from submitting to this given social reality and gives them the power to change things. While the immediate concern of the author is, of course, the place and activity of women, her interpretation has a deeper interest for community and social change which gives a voice to any excluded from influence in human affairs.

The story she tells is indeed a story of God and of naming God. *Sophia* or Wisdom is a central image. All are accustomed, at times, to using the term of Jesus as God's Son or even of Mary's obedience and faith, so that she too earns the title of Seat of Wisdom or even Divine Wisdom. For Schüssler Fiorenza, however, the story is not just about the naming of Jesus but about the naming of God. It is God who is called Wisdom or *Sophia*, bearing all the feminine characteristics which Wisdom literature attributes to her. Jesus is, then, the prophet of Wisdom. To sum up pages of critical and revealing study, the following is cited: "This reality of God-Sophia spelled out in the preaching, healings, exorcisms and inclusive table community of Jesus called forth a circle of disciples who were to continue what Jesus did. Sophia, the God of Jesus, wills the wholeness and humanity of everyone and therefore enables the Jesus movement to become a 'discipleship of equals.'"[14]

It is not our intention to give a homogenous characterization of feminist theology. We have here recalled this work of Elisabeth Schüssler Fiorenza because it makes it very clear that any narrative contribution to the quest for justice and peace is about naming God. Much can be said and told about Jesus and about the church, but it misses the point if it is not made clear that revelation and church are about the name of God, the action and presence of God, and this has to be the fundamental motivation moving the hearts and minds of those who seek justice.

Among feminist theologians themselves the address to God as Father is disputed. A common critique is that this naming and invocation has had a role in Christian history of sanctioning forms of patriarchy, both sacred and secular. This is because the name has been used in a form which relies on concept and image, passing over its metaphoric origins in narrative and even the dogmatic insistence that within God, in whose image humans are made, there is no gender, no hierarchy, no supremacy, no domination of one over the other.

---

[14] Ibid., 135.

The meaning of a name has to be read from narrative context and even from a sequence of developing and complementary narratives. In biblical narrative the name of "Father" has not been plucked from some ordered system of relations, familial or social, but it is a name that accrues meaning from an ongoing story, in the course of which it is freed from any gender or social rigidities. The word functions symbolically, that is to say it has roots in experience, specifically in the experience of the transcendence of God. It offers readers and speakers a way of relating to God as this name helped to shape Israel's relation to the God of the covenant and creation; it then allows them to appropriate the message and the experience of Jesus in revealing God to humanity. On the lips of Jesus, turning to God as Father goes beyond an exclusive relation of the God of the covenant to Israel, extending divine love and choice to a wider humanity. In declaring Jesus "beloved Son," God is heard to show a predilection for the poor and simple who, for Jesus, have their special place in the kingdom that comes from above. It is vital to the narrative and the name "Father" to see that Jesus himself enters fully into this relation with God in his passion and on the cross, in the hour, that is, of his self-emptying, in his abandonment to solidarity with the dross of society and with the painful experience of all in facing death. Revelation of Father and revelation of justice in such a context has nothing to do with dominance.[15]

Another thing worthy of particular note is that scriptural narrative and then spiritualities offer many other ways of naming God as source, summit, and that which is more intimate to oneself and one's relations with the world than one can grasp. This is not novel. It has been present in tradition for centuries. Gertrude of Helfta in the fourteenth century, for example, is quoted as calling God "Goodness," "Omnipotence," "Friend." As we have seen from *In Memory of Her*, the Scriptures themselves provide the name of God as Wisdom. Others have pointed to how, within the story of Israel or within the story of Jesus, God is called Spouse, Mother, Shepherd/ess, Rock, or Fount of Life, all of which, for believers, have to be taken as complementary to how God is named "Father" from the mouth of Jesus because of the relation he has in his humanity to God, a relationship he shares with his disciples. Pauline

---

[15] For a feminist perspective on how Christians may continue to address God as Father, see Janet Martin Soskice, *The Kindness of God: Metaphor, Gender and Religious Language* (Oxford: Oxford University Press, 2008), 66–84.

letters use the name Father later to enable believers and communities to relate in freedom to creation, to principalities and powers both "on earth and in the heavens." The reminder is that to conceive of God's relation to the world and the world's to the transcendent, we have to keep going back to stories, to the poetic, to art, to capture how dynamic and rooted in life is the experience of being invited to name God.

With its critiques and imaginative proposals, feminist theology calls upon us to attend to the ineffability of the divine name. We might then better appreciate what was said of baptism by Justin Martyr in his first apology: "The name of God, the Father and Lord of the whole universe, is pronounced over anyone who chooses to be born again." He adds that the one who baptizes invokes this name alone, "for God so far surpasses our powers of description that no one can really give a name to him." The *coup de grâce* is then added: "Anyone who dares to say that he can must be hopelessly insane" (*Apologia* 1.61). Justin then goes on to explain the other creedal formulas of baptismal bathing when the Son and Spirit are invoked, showing that without these invocations the invocation of the Father rings hollow.

In the title of this subsection of the chapter we have used the word "redress." Redress is understood as the effort to do or bring something about which, at the same time, exacts some undoing. Any practice that ensues depends on the work of the imagination, on the way the imagination can recast the shape of the world in which people live. To perform its task, imagination in storytelling and in poetry takes reality fully into consideration but asks of it that it can be retold, remade in another fashion. Here, we cannot but be aware of how the names given to God across time have served to create a certain reality, to shape the way of things. If God is considered foundational to existence, even the very heart of one's being and instincts and wise action, it is inevitable that divine naming has a deep impact, and thus, instead of offering freedom, this can compromise with restriction, injustice, and war making. Hearing the Word and recasting the Word in story, poetry, hymn, or even community structure by way of an episcopal or regal appropriation of Divine Names, is perilous. In naming God with faith and reverence, the inner freedom of the Spirit has to be sought and constantly nourished so that the Word may set free in truth, when the Word itself is freed from the hold of ideologies and idealist systems.

Naming within Interreligious Dialogue and Collaboration

There are many ways in which faith and life are enriched for all through the dialogue and cooperation between persons of diverse faiths and religions. Here, our interest is to see how this may shape the common quest for justice, peace, and harmony with creation which Christians pursue in the name of the triune God.

In recent decades the Catholic Church and other churches have explicitly recognized that their mission is inclusive of working for the reign of God in the world among all peoples, not only among those of the Christian faith. Further, they see that, sent in the name of Christ to do this work, they are to collaborate with others, in a particular way with communities of diverse religious faiths. Bringing about alleviation of the suffering of the poor, serving the establishment of organizations that promote justice, and forging local worldwide peace often necessitates reconciliation. It cannot be done except as a human community where differences are respected and bridged in a constant interaction. What all will call the transcendent, and many religions call God, is better known in the work that humans do in this name for the cause of justice, peace, and the preservation of creation.

Respect for others and working with others, not anonymously, but with specific appreciation for what the other stands for, means getting to know one another's stories as well as their belief systems and rituals. In affirming that God has been and is at work in all peoples and through all religions, Christians have to see that this must mean for them a harmonization between their doctrine of salvation and their belief in the Trinity. With John Paul II in *Redemptoris Missio*, Catholics have retrieved elements from the texts of early Christian writers in choosing to talk of the seeds of the Word and the inspirations of the Spirit that are found in all quests for the good. They do not require others to adopt these designations, but for themselves they come to better understand what they have received as revelation when they can discern Word and Spirit at work far beyond the confines of the Catholic Church and indeed those of other Christian bodies. In the post-apostolic exhortation *Ecclesia in Europa* (nos. 18–19) John Paul II wrote of the Word of God incarnate as the presence of the infinite God at the heart of finite humanity in its struggles to find communion and unity.

Entering into dialogue with others, and seeing respect for the transcendent and work for justice wherever they are found in the light of the Word and Spirit, Christian believers deepen their faith in this triune

God and expand their understanding. In other words, it needs to be said that naming a God of peace and justice, and naming this God as Father, Son, and Spirit, has to be done within an interreligious dialogue and action that promotes this movement and quest. Not only the stories from Abraham to Jesus Christ are stories within which God is named. Seeing God in the stories of all peoples and religions when working with them for justice increases our understanding of the mystery of the Trinity.

As early as 1970, Ewart Cousins was able to say that, as a believing people, we have entered a new phase in the understanding of the mystery of the Trinity once we confess a working of the Word and the Spirit in all peoples and religions of the world.[16] Two factors then come together: First, there is a very particular way in which knowledge of God deepens and increases when we see that God is to be named, in triune revelation, as a God of justice, as a God who works in creation and in humanity to establish what we call the divine reign. Second, this presence and action takes on the physiognomy not only of Christian communities but of all those who work to establish an order of common good, peace, and tranquillity, where peoples and earth are joined in creativity and harmony.

In offering guidelines for interreligious dialogue and interaction, the World Council of Churches gave this as a theological basis for dialogue:

> In their encounters with neighbours of other religious traditions, many Christians have come to experience the meaning of a "common humanity" before God. This experience is rooted in the biblical affirmation that God is the creator and sustainer of *all* creation. "The earth is the Lord's and all that is in it, the world, and those who live in it" (Ps. 24:1). God called the people of Israel to be witnesses among the nations while, at the same time, affirming that God is the God of all nations (Ex.19:5-6). The eschatological visions in the Bible anticipate all nations coming together and the creation being restored to the fullness that God intends for all. This conviction is reflected in the affirmation that God is not without witness among any people or at any time (Acts 14:17).[17]

For their part Catholics may appreciate what was said about the spirituality of dialogue in 1998 by Cardinal Francis Arinze, then prefect of the

---

[16] Ewart Cousins, "The Trinity and World Religions," *Journal of Ecumenical Studies* 7 (1970): 476–98.

[17] "Guidelines for Dialogue and Relations with People of Other Religions: Taking Stock of 30 Years of Dialogue and Revisiting the 1979 Guidelines," *Current Dialogue* 40 (December 2002): online at http://www.wcc-coe.org/wcc/what/interreligious/cd40-04.html.

Council for Interreligious Dialogue: "The spirituality which is to animate and uphold interreligious dialogue is one which is lived out in faith, hope and charity. There is faith in God, who is the Creator and Father of the whole of humanity, who dwells in light inaccessible and whose mystery the human mind is incapable of penetrating."[18]

To this Cardinal Arinze related the hope which characterizes the Christian community when it is referred to as eschatological hope and is brought to bear on dialogue: "Hope characterises a dialogue which does not demand to see instant results, but holds on firmly to the belief that 'dialogue is a path towards the Kingdom and will certainly bear fruit, even if the time and seasons are known only to the Father (cf. Acts 1:7).'"

Readers might appreciate even more the comments of Archbishop Michael Fitzgerald, then secretary of the same council, on dedicating the last of three years of preparation for the 2000 Jubilee to God the Father. He deftly related this to the other great religions of the world in taking Pope John Paul as an example.[19] Fitzgerald remarked first how on pilgrimage to the Middle East the pope retraced the story of Christians back to the story of Abraham, who is recognized by the three monotheistic religions as father in faith, as one through whom God made covenant with humankind. Beyond this he noted how John Paul shared with Jewish brothers and sisters faith in the liberation of the Israelite peoples from Egypt and in the covenant made through Moses at Sinai.

While taking note of the importance of meeting with leaders of religions in Assisi, Fitzgerald went on to recall that the attention and solicitude and brotherly affection of John Paul II was not confined to the so-called great religions of the world but was extended to practitioners of what are called traditional religions, most especially in Africa, but also in Oceania and parts of Asia and of the Americas. Speaking to members of traditional religions in Benin, he noted the importance of the traditions they receive from their ancestors. In them is found their expression of the holy that embraces the universe as well as particular regions and places and their concern for harmonious living, their joy in celebration, and their search for an ethic that promotes peace within and among

[18] Francis Cardinal Arinze, "Spirituality of Dialogue," http://www.vatican.va/roman_curia/pontifical_councils/interelg/documents/rc_pc_interelg_03031999_spirituality_en.html.

[19] Archbishop Michael Fitzgerald, "Riflessioni sul Santo Padre Giovanni Paolo II," http://www.vatican.va/roman_curia/pontifical_councils/interelg/documents/rc_pc_interelg_doc_20050501_john-paul-ii_it.html.

diverse peoples. Without hesitation, all of this could be blended with the Christian faith in the one true, good, living, and loving Father who sent his Son and the Spirit into the world to inspire and enter into these movements of the human spirit.

In this way we can say that diverse stories and the common story of humankind in the search for a community that lives in peace and in oneness with nature, immediate and cosmic, come from the fact that all have their origin in the one source of life, in the one God, who is creator of all and the font of truth and goodness. All these stories are those of coming forth and seeking to find communion in the one living wellspring of life. In all of these stories and traditions, Christians, open to biblical signs, are invited and enabled to discern that fatherly love which, beyond the human naming of fathers, they call *agape* as this has been evidenced in one they name as Son, the image and icon of the one from whom he was sent to be an integral and redeeming force in humanity's search.

Conclusion

In this chapter we have addressed the fact that the process of naming involves narrative or story and that this has an ethical as well as a doctrinal intent. We have looked in different quarters for how the process of naming God in story relates to the quest for justice and peace. This could be completed by looking at how the naming is then carried forward through use of other literary forms such as poetry, prophecy, wisdom, and law. This, however, is a task that has not been undertaken, except by way of passing reference, while treating fundamentally of narrative. In focusing on this we have indicated how a reading of biblical stories relates the divine name to justice. We have also wanted to show how the naming continues against this background, even as peoples tell their own stories in the light of the Gospel, and what this says to a global intersubjective conversation in the interests of a global humanity which knows the importance of the particular.

Suggested Readings

Fiorenza, Elisabeth Schüssler. *Jesus: Miriam's Child, Sophia's Prophet.* New York: Continuum, 1995.
This influential proponent of feminist theology treats of how to name Jesus and how to name God through a theological hermeneutics of scriptural texts.

Gutiérrez, Gustavo. *On Job: God-Talk and the Suffering of the Innocent.* Maryknoll, NY: Orbis, 1987.
The author treats of suffering within the horizon of a mystical liberation theology.

Kelly, Robert Hamerton. *God the Father: Theology and Patriarchy in the Teachings of Jesus.* Philadelphia: Fortress, 1979.
Kelly shows how in his proclamation of the advent of the kingdom of God Jesus transformed the meaning of calling God Father.

Orobator, Agbonkhianmeghe E. *Theology Brewed in an African Pot.* Maryknoll, NY: Orbis, 2009.
In this accessibly written and insightful book, the Nigerian theologian discusses how the triune mystery is named among African peoples.

Ricoeur, Paul. "Naming God." In *Figuring the Sacred: Religion, Narrative, and Imagination*, edited by Mark I. Wallace. Translated by David Pellauer. 217–35. Minneapolis: Fortress Press, 1995.
In a hermeneutical reading of scriptural texts, Paul Ricoeur shows the potential and the limitations of naming God in narrative context and notes the importance of this naming in the present era.

Senior, Donald. *Jesus: A Gospel Portrait.* Mahwah, NJ: Paulist, 1992.
A simply written but scholarly treatment of what the New Testament tells us of Jesus in his family, social, and religious setting.

Soskice, Janet Martin. *The Kingdom of God: Metaphor, Gender, and Religious Language.* Oxford: Oxford University Press, 2008.
A feminist scriptural perspective on treatment of the biblical language of God and God's kingdom, which deals directly with what it is to call God Father.

CHAPTER 4

Ethics of Divine Justice

W e cannot speculate about divine justice according to rationally conceived notions of what a just society would look like or how justice is to be arbitrated, though these conceptions do tell us of human expectations. For example, the United Nations Charter on Human Rights is upheld by widespread agreement on what constitutes the good life and on the violations of human dignity that are intolerable. This does not, however, constitute a set of ideas to which divine justice must conform, for this we may know only by attending to what is revealed about what God wills for the good of creatures and of creation. As is sometimes said now in theologies, believers are to attend to what is made known, to the phenomena of divine gift which event and Word make manifest. It has been common for a long time in theology to speak not simply of an order of divine justice but of an order of mercy and justice, realizing that one cannot be acclaimed without acknowledging the other. More recently, in his letter *Caritas in Veritate* Benedict XVI has reminded the world that for Christian believers charity or love is the form of justice. While intellect and reason on a basis of insight into human experience may speak of expectations about authentic human development, these are subsumed by theology into an order where love and mercy and reconciliation give form to human communities and even to a human order that operates at a global level.

This does not mean that we are looking for a copybook image of justice. It takes considerable efforts of interpretation and assimilation to open mind and heart to what the story of revelation says about divine justice. There are, after all, apparently contradictory factors in the operation of that to which God calls those whom he chooses. It is impossible to turn a blind eye to the brutality meted out to other peoples and even to animals in the doings of the chosen when they see themselves as inheritors of the earth that God has given them. Beginning with the patriarchs and then with the ransom of Israel, a prevailing persuasion is that of God's choice, of divine election: it is this which dominates among the people who follow God and obey his laws. This is coupled with a sense of the concern which Israel is to have for the poor within their own communities, for the land, and indeed for the stranger. It took considerable prophetic denunciation to make the leaders and the prosperous see that neglecting the practical details of the precept of love of neighbour leads to the collapse of the entire social and civic order of life and leaves the kingdom open to assault from without. It also took the voice of Isaiah and others to bring Israel's attention to an order among nations and peoples in which mutual respect and mutual concern and much reconciliation and considerable gift of self for the sake of others is demanded of God's worthy followers and servants. The broadness of this persuasion did not appear in all its fleshly dimensions until the advent of Jesus of Nazareth, acclaimed as the Christ and Son of God. What this meant for those who professed themselves his disciples is worked out in the books of the New Testament, even then leaving much to be discerned "according to the tradition" by generation after generation of those who in the Spirit confess God as the Father of Jesus Christ. It has never been primarily external precept which governs the quest for a just society, but this results from the movement of faith within persons and within communities that is moved by the operations of Word and Spirit.

To live by divine justice is to be conscious that humanity is justified not by its own configurations of justice but by the justice whereby God justifies a sinful race. All inner-worldly systems of just ordering have to render an account of what comes as a gift from the transcendent and leads to the quest for a common humanity that aspires to communion with what is given and finds in this the ground of a human order that makes authentic human development possible. This transcendent is given a compassionate face in the person of Jesus of Nazareth, who is proclaimed as Word and Son of God. In a world that knows much sin and conflict, his teaching and his action dig deep into the fundamental aspirations of the human community.

To understand the justice of the Divine Trinity at its roots, we can look at a play between the words "just," "making just," and "order of justice," as the English language allows. Whoever is just is just because made so by God's merciful gift. Those who are just are made into a people among whom love prevails over division, life holds sway over death, and goodness strikes out sin. This is expressed in the First Letter of Peter when the author speaks to the baptized of the dignity of those who have been purchased by the precious blood of the Lamb (1 Pet 1:17-21). The order of justice, then, means reconciliation, overcoming conflicts, and breaking down barriers. Lived within the church, this becomes a witness to the world and an ambition for the world. There can be no closure within a community but a mission that is largely discerned through a diagnostics of disempowerment, dehumanization, and suppression of diversity.

First Peter speaks much of the new creation, of the new heavens and new earth to which believers look forward in hope, for this expectation completes the sense of being made just. Affirming the transcendental origin and finality of justice, however, does not take Christians out of the world into another realm but teaches them a way of living by the justice given to them. Evil is overcome and good is pursued only by looking to God's gift and God's promise, made in Jesus Christ. On various occasions Paul's letters proclaim the justification given in Christ to be the overcoming of the powers and principalities which claim allegiance even as they treat many unjustly. In the Gospel of Matthew, the righteousness of the kingdom of heaven means the ethical commitment of those who have heard the Beatitudes and seek the kingdom among the poor and the merciful. According to the Gospel of Luke the kingdom and its justice means the reversal of the fortunes of those who suffer indignity and inhuman treatment. Thus, putting on the mind of Christ, as Paul tells us we must do, means a commitment under God to aligning with the poor, and the testimony to love and to God's truth in the face of evil which is exemplified by Jesus himself.

The word "solidarity" often expresses the conditions of such a commitment. Solidarity properly understood begins with grief, with the readiness to share the sorrow of others, which allows us to see justice from within affliction. Noting Jesus' own weeping over suffering and over sin we might well say that for all of us the search for God's justice begins with grief, grief over sin and grief over what many have to endure. When the heart is not pierced, action runs the risk of becoming a pragmatic programme that turns on a humanly conceived righteousness.

The voice of a solidarity which begins in grief is lament. Lament not only embraces the suffering of humanity but extends to the whole created order. Seeing the extent of the first means attention to the second since the fate of the human race and of individual peoples is tightly bound with nature. Addressing the diplomatic corps accredited to the Holy See at the beginning of 2010, Benedict XVI connected the suffering of humans with the exploitation of natural resources and the restoration of justice with care for the environment: "I would like to stress again," he said, "that the protection of creation calls for an appropriate management of the natural resources of different countries and, in the first place, of those who are economically disadvantaged." Quoting his own message for the World Day of Peace, he asserts that the world needs to ensure "forms of agricultural and industrial production capable of respecting *creation* and satisfying the primary needs of all."[1]

In the same address, speaking quite specifically of countries in Africa and in Latin America, as well as of Afghanistan, he pointed to the struggle for access to natural resources as one of the causes of conflicts. Hence, he says, "to cultivate peace, one must protect creation." Not only does the exploitation of natural resources lead to an unequal distribution of wealth and increasing immigration from indigenous lands, but it provides for a military expenditure that uses up resources which would be better put to use serving "the development of peoples, especially those who are poorest."[2]

As a theological basis for the right use of creation Benedict offers some considerations on human freedom. He affirms the legitimate autonomy of the temporal order and the gains for all of Enlightenment concerns. Nevertheless, a true sense of freedom has to determine relations to cosmos and environment: "freedom cannot be absolute, since man [*sic*] is not himself God, but the image of God, God's creation. For [humans], the path to be taken cannot be determined by [human] caprice or wilfulness, but must rather correspond to the structure willed by the Creator."[3]

In the encyclical letter *Caritas in Veritate*, the pope teaches therefore that questions of justice have to be subsumed into the order of charity. Charity is to be practiced not only in personal relations and in family life and neighbourhood but must include relationships within social, economic, and political realities. This is to allow the whole human order to reflect the truth that "God is love" (1 John 4:8, 16). Love, however, is not to be reduced to sentimentality but is guided by truth and leads to action.[4]

---

[1] Benedict XVI, Address to the Diplomatic Corps, accessed at http://www.vatican.va/holy_father/benedict_xvi/speeches/2010/january/documents/hf_ben-xvi_spe_20100111_diplomatic-corps_en.html; emphasis added.

[2] Ibid.

[3] Ibid.

[4] Benedict XVI, *Caritas in Veritate*, 2.

A theological perspective on the protection of creation was also given by Patriarch Bartholomew of Constantinople at a symposium on ecology held at Halkj.[5] Among the reasons for protecting the environment he distinguished two basic categories. First are those that are theological and are grounded in faith. Second are pastoral reasons which inspire sensitivity to the world of creation and promote a mission of service. In speaking to the theological motivations, the patriarch invoked the persuasion of the fathers of the church that salvation in Christ is not only for the human race but, through humankind, reaches out to the whole of creation. He quotes the phrase of Irenaeus which speaks of the recapitulation of all things in Christ. He also reminds us that Maximus the Confessor described the church's liturgy as a cosmic liturgy in which, through human song and praise, all created things find a voice. All creation is destined to partake of the glory of God and of eternal life in Christ.

The Green Patriarch then goes on to list the pastoral reasons, as they emerge from the theological, for caring for the environment. Harm done to the environment, he notes, is an offence against the Creator which calls for a radical *metanoia*, or conversion, of the ways in which people relate to the environment. It is not right for humans to see themselves as proprietors of nature. They must act, rather, as priests of creation who have the duty of offering up the material world in its integrity to the Creator.

Living by Divine Justice

These perspectives enunciated by the patriarchs of East and West call for a reflection on how the order of justice envisages both humans and all of nature as they are bound to each other. This reflection is enlightened by relating the communion of divine persons and the covenants of the Judeo-Christian tradition to teachings on justice. We are asked to tease out how the twofold action of the Word and the Spirit orders the whole created order to a justice that is within the prevailing order of charity. To do this, we can look at teaching on just action and then at the respective roles of Christ and Spirit in the universe.

---

[5] *Cosmic Grace and Humble Prayer: The Ecological Vision of the Green Patriarch Bartholomew I*, ed. John Chryssavgis, 2nd ed. (Grand Rapids, MI: Eerdmans, 2009), 129–57.

Teaching on Just Action

God made covenant with the Israelite people by saving them from slavery and exile and by making God's people those who were without name. The Decalogue is offered as the practice of the chosen community in obedience to the foundational precept of love of God and neighbour. Spelling out the Decalogue, the commands of just conduct are encoded in the book of Leviticus (Lev 19:1-37) to show that right dealings with the land and with nature have to put care of the poor to the fore. This is the order of justice that is to prevail. In reaping the harvest of grain or in tilling the vineyards of the land God gave the people, enough is to be left for the poor. This is prescribed not simply as an act of benevolence but as an act of justice. There are many other such precepts concerning how to deal with the poor and the unfortunate, such as the return of the cloak that guarantees a debt. These precepts are sealed by the words, "I, the LORD, am your God." They reflect that the foundation of morality is the divine covenant rather than the conceits of mere human wisdom.

In the teaching of Jesus, the ethical norms of God's kingdom are embodied in the Sermon on the Mount, which the evangelist deliberately parallels with the revelation on Mount Sinai. The ways in which people live together and relate to others are to show forth the perfection of the Father (Matt 5:8). They are to demonstrate, as it were, the divine predilection for the poor and for those who serve peace and mercy and for those who break through barriers that keep apart. Love is to extend even to showing love for enemies.

It is the practice of Jubilee as lived out in Israel and as retrieved by Jesus in his proclamation of the kingdom which determines the order of divine justice that is the order of this kingdom. At the beginning of his mission in Galilee, when he spoke in the synagogue of Nazareth, Jesus borrowed the words of the prophet Isaiah to show that he was sent to redress the misfortunes of people and of the land itself among his own people (Luke 4:16ff.). By this particular care he made manifest a universal pattern of conduct.

This teaching of the law and the teaching of Jesus was brought home to us in 2000 when Pope John Paul II declared the purpose of the Jubilee Year to be a retrieval of the practice of Jubilee in Israel. For the Israelites, every seventh year was to be a sabbatical year and every fiftieth, a Jubilee. These were years when the people to whom it had been confided were reminded of the need to care for the earth, not to overuse it, not to exploit it beyond its natural giving. They were also years when communities were to be mindful of the poor, when land was to revert to those who may have lost it, when the command was recalled of letting the poor live from the land that landowners tilled and reaped, from the olive groves and the vineyards which they dressed. The pope noted that the sense of Jubilee should be inherent in the Christian era to every Sabbath gathering, to every coming together of a congregation for the Day of the Lord.[6]

Role of Christ in Creation

After the expression of the church's attitudes to society and creation in *Gaudium et Spes* we find the church taking consciousness of this in its way of praying. To give but one example, in the three new eucharistic prayers of the Roman Missal, Jesus Christ as Word and Son is remembered for his part not only in redemption but "in the beginning," in creation. In conceiving of an order of justice in which the restoration of world and humanity go together, the church is inspired by what is taught of the role of Christ in creation as God's ongoing work.

In the New Testament, the encounter with Christ in his lordship is an encounter with the truth of creation (Col 1:15ff.). In all that Paul says of Christ's relations to the powers of the cosmos and of the world, we perceive anew the role of the Word and of the Spirit in the work of creation and how only they give true harmony to a just and loving order of cosmic and earthly reality. In the Creed we profess that the Father of Jesus Christ is Creator. He brought things into being by the same Word by which redemption is given because God so loved the world. He is present in the work of creation and in its orientation to a harmony to be found only in God, within the divine communion of operative Word and Spirit with the Father. God spoke and so it was. This is the refrain within the Genesis narrative of creation, a narrative of an action that culminates in the creation of humankind as image of God but that terminates in the repose of God, in God's restful communion with creation, to be constantly celebrated in Sabbath and restored in Jubilee.

A true anthropology, a true understanding of the human as the image of God, is found in Christ. Humans enjoy life with and in God in the midst of creation, as friends and servants. Their role is to serve the restoration of creation, as Christ did. Humanity's freedom is to work within freedom

---

[6] Pope John Paul II, *Tertio Millenio Adveniente*, Apostolic Letter, 9–12. On the meaning of the Jubilee and its pertinence to contemporary questions, see Hans Ucko, ed., *The Jubilee Challenge: Utopia or Possibility? Jewish and Christian Insights* (Geneva: WCC Publications, 1997).

of the divine energies in the universe. As we have seen this expressed by von Balthasar, the drama of God's Word in the world is always the drama of the encounter and, unfortunately, conflict between two freedoms: the infinite freedom of God manifested in his acts of creation and love and the limited freedom of the human which is fulfilled in communion with Christ in the service of creation. Humanity risks serving narrower purposes in the way in which it uses rather than serves the riches of the natural order. The service of the order revealed in God's Word is the restoration of an order subverted by an order of sin, but it offers hope for the future.

Spirit and Creation

Liturgy, catechesis, and theology over recent years have come to an improved grasp of the role of the Spirit in the work of Christ and in the life of the Spirit. Nevertheless, we do not always see how closely this is linked with the action of the Spirit in creation. To ignore the cosmic dimension of the presence of the Spirit has dire consequences for openness to the work of the Spirit in human activity and in the restoration of justice. When he wrote of creation and of divine causality, Thomas Aquinas expected his readers to be as attentive to finality as to origins. The understanding of divine action in the world, in the giving of being, comes clear to us when we see to what it is ordered. The Spirit is the divine gift which draws earth and cosmos into the perfection of divine being. Knowing the presence of the Spirit in all of creation helps us to see all truth, beauty, and what is expressed of the relation to the divine in cultures, as the work of the Spirit.

The cosmic dimension of the presence of the Spirit is inherent to what Catholics call the sacramental principle of the created order. In looking at the universe, they have a vision of reality which comes from an understanding of liturgy as sacrament of the mystery of Christ, the invisible made visible. Without the breath of love, we cannot see and we cannot hear. Conversely, without the breath of love, the work of the Word in ordering creation to its end is unthinkable, not just in the human heart, but in all the work of creation.

This ecological consciousness is necessary to humanity's just activities in the world. Stewardship is improperly understood when thought of as use of nature's resources to serve human ends. It is, rather, the stewardship which sees its role as service of the inner ordering of the whole household of being. Seeing this as the work of the Spirit who is present to us and to creation gives us an appreciation of the world as it comes forth from a single life-giving divine act of self-communication which in its wisdom and in its vital élan is one harmonious work. If the Spirit now groans within us as we hear creation groan, this is because we come to know that the world is enmeshed in a web of exploitation where the lives of many humans and the resources of nature are exploited for the supposed well-being of the few.

It is the eschatological Spirit, the pouring out of the Spirit in these messianic times, which is the root of what we call the eschatological orientation of all existence by which hope is kept alive. It is the Spirit as an ordering of love which enables us to see that the world is given its meaning and purpose in a transcendental orientation, in the ordering of all to the glory of God, but which sees that energy at work now in the way that things are ordered in a justice of love, in a justness of love.

Kenosis

The revelation of the truth of God's love and justice in world and creation is made manifest in Christ's *kenosis*. The power of this Word at work in the world restoring all things cannot be properly grasped without a reflection on this as something which has its ground in God's own love and generosity. We learn not just that God loved the world but that he so loved it that he gave his only-begotten Son and, having delivered him to death and then raised him up, he poured out the Spirit in abundance on human flesh.

The story of Jesus Christ as evoked in the hymn of Philippians 2:6-11 is, in effect, a culmination and assimilation of all that precedes the story of God's covenant with his people for the sake of the world. The complex narrative of God's alliance, the gift of God's law that is based on the law of love of God and neighbour, God's prophetic reminder of a justice that brings relief to the poor and suffering, and God's love of creation reach a climax in the preaching, death, and resurrection of Christ. It is there that the name of God as Father, Son, and Spirit emerges. The image of *kenosis* provides a key to interpretation, whose social or even political implications appear when we look at it in the context of a confrontation with and a critique of the powers that dominate the world.

In reading the Philippians hymn the French philosopher and theologian Stanislas Breton suggests[7] that a good place to begin in reading the

---

[7] Stanislas Breton, *The Word and the Cross*, trans. Jacquelyn Porter (Fordham, NY: Fordham University Press, 2002).

text is with the word *doulos* or "slave." The Christ of God, the one sent by God, took on the form of a slave. Despite what is often said in a long history of comment on this text, the term is not simply applied to the incarnation of the Son, to the fact that he took on a humanity enslaved by sin, but reflects the condition he embraced within the world of human beings. The Christ appeared at the lowest rung of the social order, in a form which divorced him from freedom and power. He went further and allowed himself to be given over to death, even the humiliating death on a cross. He was given not the death of a freeman but that of a slave, of one who dies outside the walls of the city because he is deemed to have lived outside the boundaries of legitimate society.

The act, however, in its very location outside the pale, is presented as active obedience to another order of things intended by God and so as generous gift, as testimony to divine *agape*. This is why Breton allies the reading of the image of self-emptying, or of making nothing of self, with what Paul says of the power of the cross in 1 Corinthians 1:21-25. The cross as the power of God and the wisdom of God excludes from its conception forms of human wisdom and religious legalism or visionary apocalyptic. God does not act or speak as we would expect. All forms of wisdom and power which claim to represent God, or even enduring ideas and ideals, are called into question. Facing humans, in the missions of Word and Spirit, God, out of abundant love, is prepared to empty the divine self in such a way that it appears as nothing in the world. He echoes love out of this abyss, but in so doing invites companionship, loving communion, and an awesome re-creation, embodied in a power outside the ordinary measures of power in religious and secular associations. Humanity can be made new, but from another place, by another speech, by a testimony to the force of love which is contrary to the ordinary forms of the exercise of power and the wisdom of the mind.

By reference to the sayings and deeds of Jesus and to the passion narrative, it is not difficult to flesh out the mystery of *kenosis* in trinitarian as well as social terms. The first act of Jesus after his mission by the Father, when he is overwhelmed by the gift of the Spirit, is to contend with Satan, with the religious, economic, and political powers allied with evil. Throughout his life, he is seen in contention with the prevailing power of those who interpret the law and put to him their trick questions about such things as marriage, divorce, and the payment of the tribute. In the passion narratives, we see the meaning of the testimony to God given by Jesus when we see that his opponents are those who stand for the prevailing religious and political power embodied in the Sanhedrin, the priests, Herod, and Pilate.

In the drama of Christ's self-emptying, in his very being as Son and image of the Father and acting in the gift of the Spirit, or in his making nothing of himself, the whole drama of humankind's use of power is acted out. Arraigned before the powers of the world, he is caught in the perplexity of power over the self that is challenged by obedience to the Father. In the name of Lord given to the one who passed through the cross, and on the cross became the bolt that holds the universe together, challenge is made to the order of things subjected to power. Before temporal and religious rulers, there is revealed a whole different kind of power that resides in the Godhead and enlightens the world that he has so loved. What is exacted here is the exercise of power rooted in *agape* and the justice of divine forgiveness and reconciliation, a power which, to be established, has to empty itself out before the world and empty itself of all our customary denominations of power.

This revelation of godly power in the drama of Christ is a response to the Eve/Adamic drama of wishing to be "like God," of choosing to be at the axis of the separation of good and evil, of wishing to be the autonomous founding couple. But they fail to see the gift, the given, the goodness that arises from the divine creative word that sees that all is good. Fascinated by their particular tree, they miss the beauty of the universe and the life that is in all things that come forth as gift from God. This is not, of course, to describe a scientific explanation of origins but the mode of being of things in their beauty which calls for the capacity to be in admiration of whatever scientific exploration and explanation unmasks for us. The one who is the Word, through whom all was made, adopts the figure of a slave in counterpoint to the couple which wished to be in the world as the race that dominates.

The Cry of the Poor

As said above, many of the issues which emerge in looking at the conditions of poverty, even within the perspectives of secular society, have begun to gravitate toward the problems raised in the exploitation of the environment. For Christians this means that in hearing the cries of the poor we hear also the cry of the earth and, with this, the voice of Word and Spirit. In ordering justice and in seeing it as a divine justice of trinitarian presence, we must start today with the cry of the poor. Bringing the Good News of

Jesus Christ to diverse peoples in our time belongs within the significance of the "today" which liturgical memorial celebrates, proclaiming that this day, in our eyes, the mystery of God's love is made known and active.

With Pope John XXIII, the Catholic Church defined its mission anew in terms of the option for the poor, and this continues to be a common phrase in magisterial documents and in theologies. Its full implications are, however, being continuously worked out. With the document on the church in the world (*Gaudium et Spes*) of the Second Vatican Council, the magisterium in the name of all disciples of Jesus pronounced a strong commitment to justice for the poor and to their integral human development. When CELAM discussed this at Medellin in 1968, they spelled out the call to serve communities of the poor so that they themselves would be agents of faith and evangelical freedom and their voices would be heard in the interpretation of the Gospel message of Jesus. At Aparecida, some forty years later, the same conference gave primacy to the supporting of self-sustaining indigenous communities on the lands and in the waters that were those of their ancestors and on which they lived in vivid communion with the environment.

When we talk today of the poor now we see how their profile is being shaped by developments in a global world that inflict fresh impoverishment because of the exploitation of natural resources, as we have seen this spelled out by Benedict XVI. The results of the global interaction which indulges in exploitation are felt most poignantly in local realities, and the word "glocal" aptly expresses how global problems are felt in particular places around the world, affecting not only people's standards of living but also their cultural identity.

The pertinence of a divine order of restorative justice is grasped even better when we hear Jesus speak in the Spirit in Nazareth, citing the Jubilee proclaimed in the book of Isaiah. Jesus addresses what Jubilee is to mean, what a whole order of divine action described as Jubilee when the Spirit is at work could mean. He addresses himself to the Galileans in how they suffered in their bodies and in the lands from the exploitation of the foreign invader and of the Herodian kings and from the taxes levied by the temple priesthood. Galilee is the world in miniature, the ways in which the lives of the poor are affected and how in God's Jubilee hope is to be restored to them.

The eschatological horizon of belief in Christ is renewed in face of global developments. It is crucial to keep in mind Jesus' appeal to the prophetic announcement in Israel of the coming of the kingdom. The

God of the universe is known to us in the presence in this world of the compassionate Christ and the enabling power of the Spirit that relates all peoples and all things in a communion of love. Whatever the future of the cosmos or of the human race on this planet, the promise of God's love and of God's life is given to us in the person of Jesus Christ as he lived among the people of Galilee in their struggle with nature and with the powers of this earth that threatened their existence while pronouncing them blessed. Our efforts to be respectful of nature and to steward its resources are important, but they will not be a guarantee that the order known to us will survive the movement of cosmic energies. Yet we keep believing that human destiny is intertwined with the destiny of the universe and that Christ's lordship, or our vision of the Cosmic Christ, embraces the whole of reality within the single love of the Creator God.

Word of the Weak

For the sake of an order of justice for humanity and cosmos, we have to restore power to the weak. Poverty (material and cultural), alienation, and conflict are rooted in a pervading dualism in perspectives on the material and bodily world. Elisabeth Schüssler Fiorenza offers the image of an alternative community, the Sophia Community, of the followers of Jesus, the one who is an expression of the Divine Wisdom that orders all things, but here we may turn to Rebecca Chopp in what she has written on the power to speak.[8]

One could dwell long on this drama and its revelation of true power, power in truth, always pointing to Jesus as the Word of God made known to us in the breath of the Spirit. What does this breath-taking and breath-giving word say of human discourse, in the ways in which it both masks the divine reality and lays open possibilities for speech and for life? Rebecca Chopp, in her book titled *The Power to Speak*, writes of how in the Word made flesh the power of word is restored to the speechless of the world. In hearkening to the Word who is Jesus, Chopp goes to the root of all critique of structures and all creative contribution to a more just order through a critique and exploration of the power of language, speech, and, fundamentally, God-talk. This is no simple matter of introducing feminine images into images of the Trinity, or of how words in the Scriptures need to be translated, or of inclusive language. It is to ask

---

[8] Rebecca Chopp, *The Power to Speak: Feminism, Language, God* (New York: Crossroad, 1991).

in effect a root question: where do speech and language originate, from what sources do they spring, and how are they so often manipulated?

In the ordering of society, the word most often heard is that of those at the centre of power, of those whose position is confirmed by the dominant symbols of public order and social life. The Word spoken by Jesus as God's Word, and the power of speech which he offers, concerns those who are at the margins of society. They are not often given the language to express and tell of their experience, or if they speak, it is of things that are not embedded in the symbols and orderings of how all things hold together.

How we talk about God, and about Father, Word, and Spirit, is deeply involved in the critique of social order. It is not so much a retrieval of the historical Jesus and the Jesus community that Chopp seeks as a retrieval of the power of the Word which is located in the liberating experience of the Spirit. The power to speak this Word is brought to the margins of society and to those who are usually left out of God-talk. This is how God has spoken and still speaks: within the economy of human redemption as this affects all spheres of human living.

The process of thinking and speaking in virtue of this open Word is illustrated by Chopp through a reading of Luke 4:16-30. It is in the power of the emancipating Spirit that Jesus proclaims the Word of freedom, the good news of salvation. He does so "this day," stepping outside the ordinary calculations of time to invite the reader to step into an awareness of cosmic time and of the disruptive time of *kairos*, God's acting. In so doing, he disrupts the time marked out by Sabbath observance and other legal structurings. The reader, or the reading community, is set down in another space, a space occupied by those who are liminal to human society and human enterprise: the blind, the lame, the sinner, the publican, the slave, and indeed in his society many women, who then took to following Jesus as disciples.

The proclamation made by Jesus demands a confession of faith and a testimony from hearers which is quite disruptive. He is not being heard "in his own country" or by his own kin. His voice is like that of the prophet Elijah who went to the widow of Zeraphath or of Elisha to whom God sent the Syrian, Naaman. This says much as to where God's Word is sent and where the Spirit breathes among those who hear and from where the testimony to this triune presence in the world is to be given.

Though Chopp does not make the connection, this Word and the power to speak given through the Spirit relates to the metaphor of *kenosis* as it has been presented above. Just as Jesus associated himself with slaves in his moment of death, so in his preaching he goes to those who are sinners and publicans, those outside the law. He shows them where true life is found and where the vision of God's reign of justice lies. Though he speaks, as the people say, with authority, he lays aside the trappings of authority. He is neither priest nor Pharisee nor scribe well-versed in interpretations of the law. There is nothing royal about his appearance. He is carpenter's son, Mary's child, offspring of the village of Nazareth. This nothingness is basic to the power of what he says and of those to whom he addresses himself, as it is to his constant critique of scribes and Pharisees. For Chopp, the open Word of the Gospel is a word for the world, not only for the church community, but it must sound out from those to whom the Gospel is given. However helpless people may feel in face of hunger, of the apparent absence of God in their life's blood, of the forces of nature to which they feel subservient, they are rendered free when they can speak Christ, God's Word, in their own language and find him among their own peoples, in their own stories and myths and poetry.

If the churches are to be a witness in the world to divine justice and to the speech that is enabled through the Spirit's impulse to speak the open Word, they must first live this reality in their own communities and facilitate it by their own structuring. On the northern continents, we may be somewhat naively fascinated by a mythology of base Christian communities at work in the south, but for all that, the reality and hermeneutic of such a way of being church is essential. It is one which has an important purpose of giving voice to the lesser of society. It is not only that they hear the Word at that place where the Word and the Spirit descended to empower all flesh, but they speak it and the whole community of faithful is called upon to listen.

In connection with the powers of the weak, Professor Michel Beaudin of Montreal has made some telling proposals about the pastoral engagement of the church as a community on the social scene.[9] Engaging all the faithful, and the socially marginalized in particular, as community—parochial, neighbourhood, and diocesan—the church needs to hear their voice and enable them to speak and organize movements that give them entry to the social, economic, and political future making of town,

---

[9] Michel Beaudin, "Pour une ecclésiologie et une pastorale face au néolibéralisme," *Le néolibéralisme. Un défi pour le christianisme* (Ottawa: Novalis, 1995), 16–52.

countryside, city, nation, and world. The pastoral work and community organization of the church today needs to give an important place to the voice of the poor, the oppressed, and the ignored and to enable them to work together for social and political change.

For this reason, taking the risks of globalization into account, the church has to challenge the new world order to heed the voices of the poor who are reduced in existence by reason of progress and the exploitation of nature. We must note that human salvation, the redress of a world order, is bound up with our commitment to the transformation of the material and earthly realities and to the creation of a new society. Just as our faith itself is ultimately the grace of God with which we cooperate, so too the divine gift of salvation is woven into that very texture of involvement with which we attempt to change the conditions of exploitation, poverty, and misery affecting our sisters and brothers.

To be able to understand God's revelation in the past, it is necessary that it is read in light of the present of God and the signs of the times. Even more, it is a call to take seriously the God who comes into our life ever afresh and to respond to his call every time creatively and innovatively. In other words, our present world and history is not a stage where we simply enact a play already written; God encounters us afresh to become a source for transformation of our world and ourselves. That is why reading the signs of the times becomes so very vital in discovering the call of God. As noted by writers like Wilfred of India and Gutierrez of Peru, action for justice has its roots in the mystical tradition of Christianity. The Christian spiritual and mystical tradition has always seen the image of Jesus himself in the suffering person, the poor, the victims. If the poor and the suffering represent Christ, what follows is that we need to reverently listen to their voice directed to us from the abyss of poverty and suffering. This is the way to keep our faith alive, love burning, and hope imaging the new. Like the crucified Jesus on the cross, the poor speak to us, and we can understand their words—which are often a stunned silence and other times a loud cry—only when we have identified ourselves with them. It is in this sense that in the experience and in the theologies of communities of less developed peoples we find the verification of what Breton sees as the revelation of the Wisdom of God—that wisdom that orders a restoration of voice and power to the voiceless and powerless—on the cross of Jesus of Nazareth, most fully God's Son and Word in that moment.

Evangelical Perspective on Public Service

In light of the above, we have to say that a justice that flows from God's self-communication asks of believers that they find their place on the public scene in the promotion of a more just society. One could always talk of the virtue of justice as something which has to do with one's relation to family and with exercising responsibility in the workplace. If we have to see the exercise of justice as something restorative, as a public concern with promoting an integral human development for all, we have to think of what this means in a common and public agenda. Public service covers several fields, including social services, economics, and politics. Rational thinking often finds that religion has no connection with these areas of human realization, other than the general obligation to allow freedom of religious practice where this does not harm the public domain. An evangelical perspective, however, argues that these areas should also carry the imprint of a religious outlook, if this is properly understood.

The French writer Stanislas Breton, already mentioned, profiles Paul[10] in a way which shows how in the wisdom of Jesus Christ he establishes an ethic for life within a social scheme held together by religion, philosophy, and law. Whatever the restrictions set by necessities of social life, Paul wrote of a freedom and a universality of communion beyond these orderly necessities which sows the seed for changing them from within. The universal law of love by self-gift is made to undergird the ways in which people come together unhindered by the pretensions of religion, of wisdom, and of political regime while yet respecting whatever service to the whole and to the common good these may render. The letters of Paul in effect testify to an ethic of *kenosis* or self-emptying which shows how these constrictions may be overcome in the interests of what is most fundamental in human being and communion. The letters testify to an ethos of communion and service which Christ's disciples can witness to within any religious, philosophical, or legal claim.

Writing to Jews of justification by faith, Paul appeals constantly to the figure of Abraham. He shows how the figure of Abraham as type of faith in Jesus Christ brings to the surface a gratuity and a potential universality which surmounts what is given in the Torah even as it fulfils it in what is most fundamental to the covenant. This is the gift of freedom in the

---

[10] Stanislas Breton, *Saint Paul* (Paris: Presses Universitaires, 2004).

Spirit which is prior to the law and operates in all systems. Law serves to build up society by serving this more fundamental upsurge of life.

Writing to Greeks, Paul shows how the desire for the freedom to be truly human is made possible, not by looking beyond time or above the heavens, but by living within history and within the cosmos, once, as children in the Spirit, people look to God as Father who is creator and destiny of all. In this they are freed from all fear and from all attempts to reach to a wisdom which is above the earth and outside of time since true wisdom has been revealed in the scandal of the flesh and the cross of Jesus of Nazareth.

Writing to citizens of Rome, Paul writes to those who look to the large and apparently universal juridical system of the empire whose ambition is to hold all peoples together under the one jurisdiction, socially and economically. Paul offers in Christ, under the one universal Father, the possibilities of living within this or any jurisdiction but yet overcoming all boundaries, whatever their binding force. The outreach in love can pass beyond the confinement and the universal pretensions of human systems of law to attain a true universal communion. In other words, in Christ there is a truth and a bonding and a communion which is more fundamental than the effort to create a universal juridical order. Christians are harbingers of time as universal expectation and show that order is but an aspiration to a greater expectation of divine reign, the nature of which they reveal in their own flesh by drawing together all classes, cultures, ethnicities into the one communion of self-giving by self-emptying in love. As the small remnant, they live within the time given to the powers of the earth, but in their conduct they testify against any public order that is achieved at the expense of those ground down as enemies or who are regarded as superfluous persons or as nonpersons who exist outside the proclaimed identity of citizen or free. Of that which is nothing, in Christ God has made something, a something which speaks to universal truth and freedom.

With Breton's reading of Paul, one could connect a reflection on the supper and passion story in John's gospel (John 13–19). After the testimony of loving service that he gives to his disciples in the washing of the feet, Jesus testifies to the Father in the Spirit. He testifies to his followers of the Father's love, and he testifies to the true God in his trial before his judges. He is the Word of the Father who makes known his intimacy as Son. He speaks to all of the loving communion by which he and the Father are bonded in the Spirit. It is in this communion that believers are invited to share, a communion from which none are excluded and all are included. This is what is most foundational to human life, the abundant life that the Father gives them. Before his accusers, Jesus testifies that this life cannot be constricted, that it is held in check by no religious, legal, or political authority.

The Spirit who speaks through Jesus and through his disciples convinces the world of sin, of justice, and of judgment. This is what he and they say to the world: sin is to prefer death to life, darkness to the light, self-interest to a wide communion of loving embrace; justice is to remain faithful to the Father of all by being one with all in love and service; judgment is to turn back judgments against the truth on the judges who convict those who transgress the boundaries they have set. True love and service are wider than human boundaries and give witness to the one origin and the one destiny of all in the same loving Father. Living by this ethic, Christians assume economic, social, and legal responsibilities to regulate what is most immediate to the necessities of human life and order, but they inspire life in common with an impetus which reaches beyond such order.

By his reading of the letters of Paul, Breton has helped to open the door to a collaborative dialogue with Enlightenment and post-Enlightenment thinkers, alert as he is to the failures of the prevailing systems of thought and order, to contribute to a genuinely human globalization. In Breton's Paul, readers can find a critique from within these orders which makes it possible to break through them, or to deconstruct their pretensions from within so as to give priority to that which is most fundamental to human being and its desires or aspirations. Christian faith as such does not offer a social, political, or economic order, but it reveals a way of living critically, prophetically, and creatively within existing orders because of what may be called its theological or God-centred anthropology.

The purpose of all social or public services is to render life for all humanity possible, to serve the needs and rights of individual persons and of identifiable human groups, and to contribute to the interests of what is called civil society, that is, the possibility of engaging in communal and social activities that enhance the quality of life. This all means that economists, those in social service, and politicians at all levels have to continually define and redefine the concept of the common good. From the point of view of a religious outlook on life, one would say that concern with the rights and quality of human life and a sense of the common good is not possible without a sense of the transcendent. In human terms, transcendence has to do with human destiny and includes some affirmation of human origins that is beyond the capacity of humanity itself to have given. It is the transcendent which ultimately gives dignity to the human person and to a communion of life and therefore prompts a commitment to the good of the present life.

We do not want to think of a church that in Christ's name controls the public agenda. On the other hand, it is insufficient to see church communities as alternate models of society, placed rather marginally on the edges of public life, with a lifestyle that serves as critique of secularization and of injustice. It is a better perspective to say that Christians, individually and in supportive communities, take their place alongside others in the promotion of a just society while influenced or inspired in the stand they take by their faith in the triune God. This allows them to see humanity called to participate in the life of the God from whom creation flows and to communion with which we are destined. The promise of an eternal future is not the promise of a reward to those who endure suffering, nor is it simply a consolation for those who now grieve. It puts a mark on how we should now live together, in virtue of the eternal life that has come to us through the Son by the very fact of God's gracious gift: humans now have eternal life and live and work together in the hope of having it more abundantly. When we think of this in faith as the life of the Word and of the Spirit now flowing within us, shared among us, and enhancing all areas of life, we have a prestigious vision of the human community and so a sense of calling, of an inspiration from within God, in the service of the human community.

Since evangelization has to do with making known the life of God that is within humanity and gives humanity its destiny and its dignity, the role of faith in public life belongs as an integral part of witness to the Gospel, because public service is a service of that which is deepest in the human person and of the bonds of human community, interpersonal and collective, thereby extending to all social bonds. The effect of a Gospel ethic on social life is therefore at the heart of making the Gospel known and belongs within the horizon of those who see the love of God at work in all domains of life through the sending of the Word and of the Spirit.

Kingdom Values/Virtues

In pursuing the good as a communal and social endeavour, we always have to turn to how in practice things are ordered and see how this may reflect the trinitarian foundation of justice. The moral theologian Enda McDonagh has said that political theology, or a theology concerned with transforming the political and social order, has to be built around four kingdom values that intersect and complement each other.[11] These are justice, freedom, peace, and truth. The words can already stand for a broad agreement among philosophers and politicians as to what should be pillars of an emerging internal community of peoples. The question for McDonagh and for us is how they would be conceived and spelled out in a society which takes its inspiration and its ethic from the Gospel, guided by Word and responding to the movements of the Spirit in the human heart.

Justice may be commonly understood in a modern human order as that which provides all with the basic needs of life, now defined to include education, the right to worship, and a rightful say in politics and social organization in all spheres of life. Christians develop their view according to the gospel maxim that the last shall be first, the least as the one who is the greatest (Matt 20:16; Luke 9:48). In practice, this means an order where the promotion of human development among the most needy in society is a ruling principle of social order. The guarantee of freedom of choice, free speech, and the pursuit of the good is part of the legal and political code of many peoples today. Christians agree with this but think outside the boundaries. For them, the imagination of freedom and its translation into the practical order is built on what we know of divine freedom, of God's choice in sending Word and Spirit to bring new life, to communicate a share in his own glory, even at a great cost. Freedom is then exemplified in the choice to give of the self to the other, to put oneself in a deep inner freedom of heart at the service of others.

Nations and peoples and religions are growing more and more in the capacity to build a harmony of peoples, a world that knows a peace built on justice. This has to be an inner and an outer peace and a readiness for reconciliation. When Christ augurs peace to his disciples entrapped in fear after his death and burial, he speaks first and foremost of an inner peace, of a divine gift that has its dwelling place in the heart. It is the peace which as Paul says in Romans 8:1ff. drives out fear. It is trust in God and in his Son, the basis of freedom and of testimony to the truth, and the base for action in behalf of peace in the public order. As seen, this

---

[11] Enda McDonagh, *The Gracing of Society* (Dublin: Gill & Macmillan, 1989).

is a meeting point in the dialogue between followers of other religions and Christians: when one's heart is free of self-interest and of fear, then one learns the virtue of compassion and the capacity to serve others and the common good in freedom. Reconciliation becomes possible in building peace when the participants are not worried about consequences for themselves, about what their actions may provoke by way of hate or repudiation on the part of others.

When peoples ask for truth and the pursuit of truth, they may, properly, have some formulated veracities or facts in mind. Beyond these, however, they must know that truth is never encapsulated in this way and that it is a venture as much as an acquisition. As the Talmudic commentator and philosopher Emmanuel Levinas puts it, in the quest for truth one has to look into the face of the other and be put to the test in so doing. Pursuing truth is an ethic, an ethic of forgetting self to allow life for the other, to let go of one's small arsenal of truths to open oneself to consider what others say and think and do. The pursuit of truth requires conversation and dialogue. What John Paul II said of dialogue on various occasions belongs within the definition of truth. As he put it in the encyclical *Ut Unum Sint*, "the capacity for dialogue is rooted in the nature of the person and his dignity."[12] The human person and human communities cannot reach self-realization without dialogue, so that dialogue is indispensable to human communication. The pope adds, "Although the concept of 'dialogue' might appear to give priority to the cognitive dimension (*dia-logos*), all dialogue implies a global, existential dimension. It involves the human subject in his or her entirety; dialogue between communities involves in a particular way the subjectivity of each."

Forgiveness and Reconciliation

If there is to be dialogue there must be reconciliation, and without dialogue there is no reconciliation. When the bishops of Africa and Madagascar met in synod in 2009, they saw it as their call to answer to the needs of justice and peace. This could not be done without promoting reconciliation among peoples hostile to each other for reasons reaching into the past. A model for such work from their own recent history was found in the Truth and Reconciliation Commission put in place in South

[12] John Paul II, Encyclical Letter *Ut Unum Sint*, 28. Accessed at http://www.vatican.va/edocs/ENG0221/__P7.HTM.

Africa in the aftermath of an era of apartheid. Without speaking the truth as fully as possible, grievances cannot be addressed. Without a readiness to forgive, peoples cannot forge one common society in which all have a place. Without redress of injustices spoken and acknowledged, there is no way forward. Forgiveness is integral to forging a just society and a just community of peoples.

The scriptural and christological roots of this approach are found in what is proclaimed of the Son's coming into the world and spilling his blood so that enemies have been reconciled and barriers which divide broken down. With the eschatological hope of the kingdom, there is a way to look toward the reconciliation of all things, of all peoples, of all powers of heaven and earth through and in Jesus Christ when, by the work of the Spirit, his image is brought to perfection in the world.

The question of forgiveness and reconciliation already finds a place in the protohistory told in the early chapters of the book of Genesis. Cain and Abel represent two different types of life, rival to each other, already in the first hours of human life on earth. Tiller of soil and shepherd of flocks, how can they live together here on earth without trespassing on each other's domain? The fratricide of Cain is not simply the murder of a brother whom he thinks God prefers but also a way to resolve rivalry by the elimination of the other. While Cain is sanctioned, he is also pardoned. He too and his offspring are to have their place on earth. Nothing is retrieved by meting out to him what he has meted out to his brother. A pardon which leads to reconciliation, to life together, offers new possibilities of life.

Divine justice originates in the divine pardon shown in its plenitude through the Son who justifies and the Spirit who frees and sanctifies. Any social construct of justice has to embrace the reality and procedures of pardon, of reconciliation of offenders with the community. It exacts a purification of memories and a restoration of just relations. This is not to narrow attention to those judged criminal and violators of common standards. It is to think of those divided from each other through mutual recrimination and through long and hurtful memories of strife and discrimination. To pardon is to say to the one who offends, "You are better than what you have done, by reason of the gifts that are within you; you have another life within you and through your life with others that may lead you along another road." To pardon is to restore relations and the possibilities of life that come through reconciliation, without suppression of difference. It is to restore unity within difference, in truth and forgiveness.

In taking account of the consequences of harmful action, the purpose is rehabilitation, not punishing. It is to seek to reestablish relations. Social systems have to include mercy and forgiveness. Paul Ricoeur once concluded an essay on love and justice with these words: "the tenacious incorporation, step by step, of a supplementary degree of compassion and generosity in all of our codes—including our penal codes and our code of social justice—constitutes a perfectly reasonably task, however difficult and interminable it may be."[13]

Ricoeur himself has pointed out that the sense of divine justice, as well as the sense of justice which God asks of his people, passing from the Hebrew covenant to salvation in Christ, may be grasped properly only in narrative and poetic context since we cannot advance if we are attached to set conceptual or legal formulations, however needed these may be in regulating the life of a society. He sums this up by showing that the exercise of the love or *agape* which has its origin in trinitarian communion and which is to be practiced by the disciples is to be inserted by them into all human discourse and action. There has to be a play between a logic of superabundance and a logic of equivalence, with the former allowed to prevail as far as practically possible.

Forgiveness, nonetheless, is not amnesia. Nor is it amnesty in the sense that harm done is overlooked, injustice treated as though not caused, persons or groups of perpetrators pardoned without having to address the evil they have done. If the Father declares them forgiven, this means that in the Son they have now, by divine grace, the power to act justly and redress wrong. To live by mercy there has to be restoration, a setting right of relations, a readjustment of orders perturbed so that suffering can be alleviated. If the Spirit prompts compassion, or if it causes the disciples of Jesus to groan with creation, it is so that they might, even in the assurance of mercy, work at cost to bring about a restoration.

That is why some talk of restorative justice. The processes of reconciliation set in motion by Jesus Christ and continued in churches culturally distinguished have to continue in such a way as to contribute to just restoration. In early forms of the sacramentalization of penance and reconciliation, a sinner, though assured to be able to live within the mercy of God, was not finally reconciled to the Body of Christ until conversion had been accomplished, until sinful behaviour had been overcome and

---

[13] Paul Ricoeur, "Love and Justice," in *Figuring the Sacred: Religion, Narrative, and Imagination*, ed. Mark I. Wallace, trans. David Pellauer (Minneapolis: Fortress Press, 1995), 329.

right relations restored. This principle has to be lived out in such a way that it is set in motion in all efforts to effect reconciliation and set up an order in which victims of injustice and all those who suffer are given the power to live out their full humanity.

Meditating on the sending of the Son into the world for redemption, there is always a temptation to think with a broad sense of universality without enough attention to the particular. A clearer link between the crucifixion of Jesus and his ministry in Galilee and Judea shows us that redemption was universal because it was first local or particular. It was testimony given and restoration brought about in face of the authorities and the woes of those specific cultural and geographical zones. Preaching and living by the Gospel, testifying to the risen Christ in the Spirit, must always take on the same visage of particularity, without which there is no true universal communion.

In this light we see the importance given to local communities in restoring order to a global economy and exchange. Restorative justice in the public order is promoted by advocates of economic and social justice who recognize the importance to people's lives of restoring the possibility of living in sustainable local communities. The promotion of sustainable local economies that make this possible looms large in the struggle for justice in the global community. In the light of the communion brought about by the divine Trinity, we see that this means not just economy but sustainable human life which allows for supportive and growth relations among people in community, as with those outside the community, and healthy relations with their immediate environment.

Conclusion

In this chapter we have sought to spell out major implications for the social order when communal human life is seen in the light of the communion restored through the work in the world of the Word and the Spirit. In particular, we have pointed to how necessary it is to integrate an understanding and a practice of *kenosis* in testifying to God's justice and in serving society. We have also spoken of what it means to hear the cry of the poor and to give them the power to speak. Finally, we addressed the issue of how forgiveness and reconciliation find their place in the practice of a restorative justice that belongs to the establishment of the kingdom of God in the world.

Suggested Readings

Chopp, Rebecca. *The Power to Speak: Feminism, Language, God*. New York: Crossroad, 1991.
This is a feminist treatment of Jesus as God's Word and of the Spirit, and the
relation of this to the weak of society, with important implications for ecclesial
and social transformation.

McDonagh, Enda. *The Gracing of Society*. Dublin: Gill & Macmillan, 1989.
This leading European moral theologian relates the theology of divine grace to
a Christian social ethics.

Ricoeur, Paul. "Love and Justice." In *Figuring the Sacred: Religion, Narrative, and
Imagination*, edited by Mark I. Wallace. Translated by David Pellauer. 315–29.
Minneapolis: Fortress, 1995.
A hermeneutical reading of biblical thought on the interrelation between love
and justice.

CHAPTER 5

Eucharist, Trinity, Justice

A
s the first document promulgated at the Second Vatican Council, *Sacrosanctum Concilium*, the Constitution on the Liturgy, provided some direction for the ongoing proceedings. With its focus on worship, it had addressed the very essence of the church as God's people and Christ's Body. It brought into better light than had been the case for some centuries that the liturgy is a participation in the mystery of Christ's Pasch and an anticipation of final assumption into the glory of God. It also highlighted the nature of the church as the communion of all the baptized, all members active in the worship and in the life of this Body. It also made it very clear that the hearing of the Word of God is a core element of liturgical celebration and liturgical renewal.

Soon after the council, however, some asked if, had *Sacrosanctum Concilium* come later in the council, *Gaudium et Spes* would have had some impact on it. Some of the proponents of liturgical renewal earlier in the century, such as Lambert Beauduin and Virgil Michel, had made it clear that they saw participation in the liturgy and participation in the apostolic life of the church to go hand in hand. This connection between worship and mission, or between worship and apostolate, was not made explicit in *Gaudium et Spes*, but in some later magisterial teaching, this connection has come into focus. In this chapter, therefore, we intend to review this teaching, to call to mind some important points in contemporary theological inquiry, and to show how what has been said in previous chapters about living the divine justice finds its heart, its impetus, and its balance in the Eucharist, which is at the centre of the entire liturgical action of the church.

Recent Doctrinal Teaching

In his encyclical on the Eucharist, *Ecclesia de Eucharistia*, Pope John Paul II brought to our attention the link between liturgy and the apostolic engagement to promote justice. Some may have thought of the eschatological orientation of the Eucharist as that which called on the church to live already beyond the concerns of this world. On this precise character of worship, however, John Paul has this to say: "A significant consequence of the eschatological tension inherent in the Eucharist is also the fact that it spurs us on our journey through history and plants a seed of living hope in our daily commitment to the work before us. Certainly the Christian vision leads to the expectation of 'new heavens' and 'a new earth' (Rev 21:1), but this increases, rather than lessens, *our sense of responsibility for the world today.*"[1]

That the mission to establish the justice of God is rooted in the Eucharist was repeated in the papal message for the Eucharistic Year of 2004–5. In our troubled world "Christian hope must shine forth," the pope affirmed. In convoking the church to celebrate a special Year of the Eucharist, he recalled the words of *Gaudium et Spes* about the place of Christ in human history: he is "the goal of human history, the focal point of the desires of history and civilization, the centre of [hu]mankind, the joy of all hearts, and the fulfilment of all aspirations."[2] This focal point of history is the focal point of eucharistic memorial.

To gloss these words one might say that herein lies the truth of the economy of the Trinity at work in our midst, for it is in the communion of the Spirit and the Father that Christ is the goal, focal point, and destiny of history. It is in the Spirit that he was sent on his mission, handed himself over to death in obedience to the Father, and was raised up to life immortal and exalted as Lord. It is in this faith and hope that churches speak of keeping eucharistic memorial, whereby the Body continually participates in the mystery of Christ's death and resurrection and whereby this salvific event is ever active among us and not merely remembered or recalled. The Spirit prompts the church to keep alive the memory of the crucified and risen One and the vision of God's kingdom of peace, justice, and reconciliation which springs from such memory. The Word of God comes alive ever anew in the eucharistic community and its living witness. He who was made flesh shows himself afresh in the fleshly reality of his members, each community in its own geographical, ethnic, and cultural particularity.

---

[1] John Paul II, *On the Eucharist in Its Relationship to the Church* (*Ecclesia de Eucharistia*), Encyclical Letter, 20; emphasis in original.

[2] John Paul II, *"Stay with Us, Lord"* (*Mane Nobiscum Domine*), Apostolic Letter, 6.

With the years that have passed since Vatican II, Christians have become more and more conscious of the fact that commitment to justice and human development must include care of the environment, its destruction being partner with the causes of material and cultural impoverishment. In relating the celebration of the Eucharist to the church's presence in the world, Pope Benedict writes in the post-synodal apostolic exhortation, *Sacramentum Caritatis*: "to develop a profound eucharistic spirituality that is also capable of significantly affecting the fabric of society, the Christian people, in giving thanks to God through the Eucharist, should be conscious that they do so in the name of all creation, aspiring to the sanctification of the world and working intensely to that end." From this he went on to show how celebration of the Eucharist illuminates human history and the meaning of the whole cosmos. If we live by what it does and signifies, as a form of life the Eucharist can foster the devotion to the world that brings about a real change in the way humans approach history and the environment. The world, the pope points out, "is not something indifferent, raw material to be utilized simply as we see fit." The promotion of its good belongs with the call to human beings to be children of God in the one Son of God, Jesus Christ (cf. Eph 1:4-12). The letter says quite emphatically, "The relationship between the Eucharist and the cosmos helps us to see the unity of God's plan and to grasp the profound relationship between creation and the 'new creation' inaugurated in the resurrection of Christ, the new Adam."[3]

In connection with this (in no. 47) Benedict recalls how synodal interventions had drawn attention to the rite of the presentation of the gifts. In this very simple gesture, he reminds his readers, all creation is taken up by Christ in the enactment of this mystery. As Benedict puts it, in Christ "we bring to the altar all the pain and suffering of the world, in the certainty that everything has value in God's eyes." The readiness to make this offering in response to the divine invitation allows us to appreciate how God invites humanity to bring God's work to fulfilment and therefore to appreciate the authentic meaning of human labour.

This attention to the material realities of the eucharistic sacrifice chimes with what he says toward the beginning of the letter, when he calls the sacrament itself and all that it communicates a free gift of the Blessed Trinity:

---

[3] Benedict XVI, *Sacramentum Caritatis*, Apostolic Exhortation, 92.

The Eucharist reveals the loving plan that guides all of salvation history (cf. Eph 1:10; 3:8-11). There the *Deus Trinitas*, who is essentially love (cf. 1 Jn 4:7-8), becomes fully a part of our human condition. In the bread and wine under whose appearances Christ gives himself to us in the paschal meal (cf. Lk 22:14-20; 1 Cor 11:23-26), God's whole life encounters us and is sacramentally shared with us. God is a perfect communion of love between Father, Son and Holy Spirit. At creation itself, man was called to have some share in God's breath of life (cf. Gen 2:7). But it is in Christ, dead and risen, and in the outpouring of the Holy Spirit, given without measure (cf. Jn 3:34), that we have become sharers of God's inmost life. Jesus Christ, who "through the eternal Spirit offered himself without blemish to God" (Heb 9:14), makes us, in the gift of the Eucharist, sharers in God's own life. This is an absolutely free gift, the superabundant fulfilment of God's promises. The Church receives, celebrates and adores this gift in faithful obedience. The "mystery of faith" is thus a mystery of trinitarian love, a mystery in which we are called by grace to participate. We too should therefore exclaim with Saint Augustine: "If you see love, you see the Trinity."[4]

It is not only the Roman Catholic Church but other churches as well that are increasingly sensitive to how, in celebrating communion in the life of the Trinity, the Eucharist entails a commitment to taking part in bringing the new creation into being. Thus, to take but one example, the Orthodox Advisory Group to the World Council of Churches, while stating that eucharistic worship is the motivating force, declares:

Evangelical witness will speak to the structures of this world, its economic, political and social institutions. Especially necessary is the witness of social justice in the name of the poor and the oppressed. . . . The church is the mouth and voice of the poor and the oppressed in the presence of the powers that be.[5]

The way in which Orthodox and Roman Catholic thought converge in relating Eucharist to the Trinity is conveyed in the study that came out of the dialogue between the Orthodox Church and the Roman Catholic Church. Suffice to cite one passage of this text:

[4] Ibid., 8.

[5] Orthodox Advisory Group to WCC-CWME, "Go Forth in Peace: Orthodox Perspectives on Mission, 1986," in *New Directions in Mission*, 224. On the social implications of eucharistic spirituality for the missionary imperative of the local eucharistic church, see also "Final Report of CWME Consultation of Eastern Orthodoxy and Oriental Orthodox Churches, Neapolis, 1988," in ibid., 239f.

> Taken as a whole, the Eucharistic celebration makes present the Trinitarian mystery of the Church. In it one passes from hearing the word, culminating in the proclamation of the Gospel . . . to the thanksgiving offered to the Father and to the memorial of the sacrifice and to communion in it thanks to the prayer of *epiclesis* uttered in faith.[6]

That this means a commitment to bringing communion in the Trinity to bear on this present life is brought out further in the same statement. It says that the communion or *koinonia* expressed in Eucharist is both eschatological and kerygmatic. That is to say that while it is an anticipation of the fullness of communion in God which is to come at the end of time, it is also a proclamation and a making known to the world of the communion of the church in the mystery of God which is realized in the present time.[7]

These doctrinal statements which we have quoted here make it clear that the Eucharist, in being a participation in Christ's mystery and sacrifice, is a participation in the life of the Trinity. Further, they are explicit on the commitment to justice which comes from such participation. This they connect in a particular way with the eschatological orientation of the liturgy. It is the very anticipation of a share in divine glory in its fullness by the whole of creation which carries the imperative of a commitment to the promotion of justice and with this of ecological equilibrium.

Sacramental Body/Bodies

With their emphasis on eucharistic commitment to justice, inclusive of care for the environment, these doctrinal teachings prompt a reflection on the sacramental Body. The most obvious thing about the Lord's Supper in New Testament tradition is that it is an offer of Christ's Body and Blood to be ingested into the bodies of those gathered at the memorial table. Since it is a celebration of the risen Christ, on the first day of the week, the Body and Blood are received sacramentally in a way that already transforms the bodies of those who receive this gift in the communion of the Spirit in whose power the Son has been raised up and is now seated at the right hand of the Father. Liturgical history shows how over the course of some centuries the focus of the celebration moved

---

[6] *The Quest for Unity: Orthodox and Catholics in Dialogue*, ed. John Borelli and John H. Erickson (Crestwood, NY: St. Vladimir's Seminary Press, 1996), 56.

[7] Ibid., 58.

from the communion rite to the offering made by the priest, so that the congregation was marginalized or made onlookers to what the priest was doing. Since Pius X and through the work of the Second Vatican Council, there has been considerable effort to bring the people back to the table and to make of eucharistic celebration a true communion of all in the one Body of Christ. At this table they receive his Body and are joined in their bodily existence with him in his communion with the Father and in the willing obedience to the Father whereby he gave over his body for the forgiveness of sins and the salvation of the world.

To grasp anew the communion of participants in this sacramental mystery which offers communion in the mystery of the Trinity in its justifying presence in the world, it is to bodiliness that attention needs to be given. Irenaeus of Lyons was among the first to reflect on the Eucharist in this way through the images of recapitulation and new creation.[8] He took a strong stance against Gnostics who thought that salvation was to rise above bodily existence and lift oneself out of any way of being beholden to the material world. As stewards of nature, those coming to the table were to bring creation itself in the bread and the wine, in which all the material world is symbolically present. In pronouncing blessing over these fruits of earth, the church anticipates its ultimate transformation promised in Christ into the new creation purified and made new in the Spirit. Ingesting this blessed bread and wine, through their communion in the risen Body of Christ the faithful knew their own bodies to be healed of sin and transformed already by the gift of immortality held sacramentally in pledge of what is to come. Preaching the goodness of creation and of the human body against Gnostic dilution of faith in the incarnation, Irenaeus was able to say that the Eucharist confirms the teaching about the goodness of creation. The core of his teaching can be summed up in this one sentence:

> Since we are his members and are nourished through creation—the creation he furnishes for us, causing the sun to rise and rain to fall as he pleases (Matt 5:45)—he declared that the cup, which comes from his creation, is his own blood, from which he strengthens our blood; and he affirmed that the bread which is from creation, is his very own body, from which he strengthens our bodies. (*Against Heresies* 5.2.2)

---

[8] The texts are readily accessible in a number of places. For example, see Daniel J. Sheering, *The Eucharist: Message of the Fathers of the Church* 7 (Wilmington, DE: Glazier, 1986), 244–52.

The eschatological expectation given to humans and to creation in living their earthly existence to the full is apparent in this teaching. Eastern theologies of the eucharistic mystery have always been sensitive to the eschatological horizon within which the whole of creation and the whole of time are seen. This relates certainly to the communion of the living and the dead in the eternal glory of the Trinity, but it also binds together remembrance of the past, expectation of the final consummation of God's kingdom, and present reality and event. This is worked out by Boris Bobrinskoy, citing both Alexander Schmemann and John Zizioulas, as well as Sergei Bulgakov, whom he quotes as saying that his "entire theological inspiration had its source in the Eucharistic cup."[9] In developing eucharistic eschatology, Bobrinskoy reminds the reader that it is in the power of the Spirit that the Word became flesh, lived on earth, gave himself over to death, and was raised up. It is also through the pentecostal flood of the Spirit that the risen Christ is present in his Body the church, both as transcending time and place and as sacramentally present in the particular reality in time and space of each eucharistic community. While including a vision of the transcendent in the eucharistic action, it involves an openness to and involvement with all communities located in a particular time and place.

The deification of humanity through eucharistic communion in the life of the Divine Trinity reaches out to the deification of all creation. Eschatological expectation is cosmic and gives great weight to the symbolism of the bread and wine as fruits of the earth, a theme already present in the writing of Irenaeus of Lyons, as we have seen. Bulgakov, as recounted by Bobrinskoy, writes of creation and then its restoration as an act of divine self-emptying or *kenosis*, which is commemorated in eucharistic communion, as the essence of the eternal relation between Father, Son, and Spirit.[10]

As Louis-Marie Chauvet has reminded us in his sacramental reading of Christian and human existence,[11] eucharistic celebration needs to be

---

[9] Boris Bobrinskoy, *The Mystery of the Trinity: Trinitarian Experience and Vision in the Biblical and Patristic Tradition* (Crestwood, NY: St. Vladimir's Seminary Press, 1999), esp. 168–73. The quote from Bulgakov is on page 147.

[10] See also Roland Jaquenoud, "Le Dieu un et trine. La personne et l'essence dans la sophiologie de Sergei Bulgakov," in *Le Christianisme est-il un monothéisme?*, ed. Gilles Emery and Pierre Gisel (Fribourg: Labor et Fides, 2001), 273–83.

[11] Louis-Marie Chauvet, *Symbole et Sacrement: Une relecture de l'existence chrétienne* (Paris: Ed. du Cerf, 1987).

attuned in ritual and in language to the intertwining of three bodies: the risen Body of Christ raised up in the Spirit and bearing the marks of the passion, the Body of the church in which he lives by the Spirit, and the body/ies of participants in which they live out their personal and social existence. We can say that this last is frequently undermined in celebration by a ritual and symbolic expression which leaves bodily life unexpressed.

The incorporation of full bodily reality, however, is essential to memory and memorial. This is the concern of the work *The Eucharist: Bodies, Bread, Resurrection.*[12] The lament of the authors is that often memorial embodies amnesia. That is to say, there is much that ought to be remembered which the very way of symbolic activity the church embraces eliminates or marginalizes. One might capture a key intuition of this work by saying that while we often associate corporate memory with the corporate community or society, memories are, in fact, carried in the physical body. Even social memories find their place of residence in the physical body, affected as it is from birth by what is passed on and by physical conditions constituted by social values and by deprivations. In maturing, a person also comes to a bodily experience of where one fits into the visible symbolic expressions of the social body. In symbolic expression, the verbal, the visual, and the ritual coalesce to express what memories are held treasured and what place they have in the symbolic code.

This can help to give hope to the wounded body or it may further degrade it. When something is omitted that is important to members of the social body, this is a sort of amnesia instead of an anamnesis. As the authors point out, something that is often left marginal to Eucharist is woman's bodily existence and experience. We know all too well that ritually women are not given readily visible and vital roles, and though there has been advance in this area since Vatican II, the matter has not yet been resolved. Their social contributions to human welfare are not well integrated into the sense of the church as Body of Christ. It is also true that with a heavy accent on commemorating virgins and on virginity, the bodily and affective experiences of bearing children and of mothering are ignored. Biblical renewal of the images of God, Word, and Spirit to include the feminine is helpful, but language is yet to be more completely transformed so that the womanly may seem not simply adjacent but essential to imaging the Trinity. In the risen Body

---

[12] Andrea Bieler and Luise Schottroff, *The Eucharist: Bodies, Bread, Resurrection* (Minneapolis: Fortress Press, 2007).

of the Lord in which those who gather share sacramentally, there is the promise of inclusion, but communities have to be open to making the promise a living part of ecclesial life.

In historical terms the divine life that emanates from the Father through the Word and the Spirit comes to be within a network of social and ecclesial relations that converge on the eucharistic table of each particular community. What is visible is visible in the Son and in turn makes the Son visible in his members. The liberating action of the Spirit frees churches from whatever ideologies or self-interests impede their openness to others, from whatever restraints on the tongue prevent them from creative speech in testimony to the Word's local and global presence. As localized peoples look out from their Eucharist to a vaster world, Word and Spirit act together to manifest a universal communion that knows the same origin and pursues a common goal.

The reconciling power of the Spirit enables communion with Christ himself in the form of otherness that he has adopted. Christ is not present in personal corporeal form but through the strangeness of word and within the space of sacramental representation. Within the Trinity of persons itself, the Spirit is often thought of as the life and love that is the communion between Father and Son in their mutual relationship. Christ, now physically absent from his church and related to it as the one who is risen and expected, lives in communion with it through the Spirit. To be present, however, in culturally expressive spoken, liturgical, and sacramental form, he is diversely present among diverse peoples, indeed diversely present even in one community when it is marked by sensitivity to peoples and cultures and diverse historical experiences. It is in the life of the Spirit and the particularity of the gifts of the Spirit that such communion is possible and real.

Eucharistic celebration is foundational to the pursuit of justice because it is the place where the followers of Christ interact as humans and where they are given the gift of the life of Father, Son, and Spirit in a divine and human exchange. It is here that Christians are given their symbolic moorings, but the symbolic needs to be renewed over time in the face of new and difficult realities, lest it be so much a testimony to a certain past it become a contemporary forgetting of what needs remembering if it is to be included in Christ.

In these times, when churches see it as their mission to be a living presence of God's own justice in the world, our multiple and varied liturgical tradition is a rich source for reflection on the relation between the mystery of the Trinity and the revelation of divine justice as divine gift. Liturgy cannot, however, be a simple reading of a word taken from the canonical text. It has to be an appropriation by a community of that word in all that it offers from within the total canon. Hearing the proclamation of the Good News of salvation in the rich variety of the biblical canon and the liturgical canon, churches transpose the address they hear from God into the naming of God in address to God, and in this find a deep consciousness of the witness to which the people are called. The Spirit at work within the community enables it to receive the Word and to give it a new contextual and living expression. According to a traditional turn of phrase, just as through the Spirit the Word takes hold, so the Spirit shines forth through the Word which becomes a living reality in the life and prayer of communities of faith.

Eucharistic Word: Putting Language on the Sacramental Presence

The eucharistic tradition is handed on to us in given and diverse forms of language and ritual, which are always subject to refashioning. Word and Spirit are at work in this tradition, giving form to remembrance as an act of a living community of faith.

To name the Trinity in the Eucharist, eucharistic language needs to be considered in its fullness. This means first attending to all of its genres, such as story, prophetic proclamation, lament, thanksgiving, and worshiping. Over and above this, it is a language which Ricoeur refers to as poetic language's polyphony of meaning and reference.[13] There is such a variety of language forms and such a harmony of images and themes that the word "polyphony" does indeed serve as apt metaphor. One aspect of this polyphony that may be underlined is that it assimilates the prophetic; that is, while at its height it is the language of memorial and of address to God, it is proclaimed in response to the primordial address of God. The church speaks the name of God only because God has first spoken to it. Prophetically, it shapes hope out of distress itself, giving a rereading of actions and words thought to have been understood but which are now disrupted through what the community suffers, putting all its confidence in God into question.

---

[13] Paul Ricoeur, "Naming God," in *Figuring the Sacred: Religion, Narrative, and Imagination*, ed. Mark I. Wallace, trans. David Pellauer (Minneapolis: Fortress Press, 1995), 223–28.

The naming and prophetic renaming of God culminates at the heart of eucharistic celebration, in the action which is the centre of gravity of all true commemoration, the symbolic action of shaping and expressing *koinonia* at the shared table.[14] In the act of receiving the gifts of the Body and Blood, there is signified and included the mutual service of the congregation to one another, in the true spirit of discipleship which is mandated in the Johannine account of the washing of the feet as the proper access to the table of Christ. It is in this typical ecclesial communion that the work of the Trinity is perfected, and it is around and from this table that the naming of God occurs.

The relation to communion with the earth and communion with one another in the goods of earth and in mutual service that is immediately expressed is essential to the ultimate referent of communion in the divine *koinonia*. As with any good symbolic expression, in the eucharistic action of a community there is an intensification of the immediately particular in the symbols of the people's own bread and wine, wrought from the earth for which they care and from which they receive care and sustenance. The immediate reference of bread and wine, of eating and drinking, may be to abundance or may be to want, as it may be to being at home or to the sense of alienation engendered by foreign foods or lack of a people's ability to provide itself with due sustenance. Such reference is not ignored or rejected, but it is suspended, and the meaning of sharing together is expressed by words and rites as a participation in the paschal and pentecostal mystery. In that communion the destiny of humankind as God's creation forms an unlimited and common hope. We can say in biblical terms that it is the experience of ecclesial *koinonia*, but this is accessible only through symbolic acts and words which receive their particular expression in geographically and culturally diverse communities and which encompass what the land means to the people and the people to the land.

In brief, then, in relation to the triune God, the language of Eucharist has several characteristics. It is symbolic in relating the communion of table and service in the church to participation in the life of Father, Son, and Spirit. It is prophetic, because the eucharistic sacrament is given to us by God through the triune action of grace, and through it God addresses us as God's own people and forms every single community as such. It

---

[14] See David N. Power, "Eucharistic Justice," *Theological Studies* 67 (2006): 856–79.

embodies a tradition that has its origins in the epiphany of the paschal and pentecostal event, and it is out of this tradition that the church has the power to live as God's people, always in expectation of the kingdom, in specific times and places. It is narrative, because revelation and divine life are given to us through the events in which God gives testimony to the love that needs no origin outside itself, and these events need to be remembered and told in order to offer their power and testimony to our lives. It is eucharistic, because we are called by God's address into relationship with the mystery of the eternal Trinity, to speak within the sacramental communion of the Body of Christ, empowered by the word that is given to us by this same Christ and moved by the Spirit to communion with him, and to make intercession for all the saints. Finally, it is doxological in the wonder expressed before the mystery of God's triune and eternal holiness.

From eucharistic rite and prayer wherein new life and hope are generated, it is apparent that the twofold mission of Word and Spirit is one in which the Word and Spirit are at work in all the actions of God in the world, from the very beginning. There is no temporal sequence to these missions, but any trinitarian theology has to account for their simultaneity and complementarity, thus avoiding the Western ecclesiastical and theological tendency to posit the mission of the Spirit after the fulfilment of Christ's Pasch, or to make it dependent on Christ, or even on the primacy of the Word, as though in some fashion the Word was sent first.

It is in the nature of God's self-emptying love to take visible form within the circumscriptions of historic event and cultural form, and by pouring forth into our hearts an indwelling of this same love. But the Word is the word of the cross, which means both the self-emptying unto death and, in the words of Stanislas Breton,[15] the crossing out of whatever human and visible forms it adopts, since they are limiting both of God and of the wisdom which is to give the divine self to the whole of creation, without limit. Paradoxically, the once and for all historic event of the cross of Christ can be given sacrament, and spoken among many peoples, only in the many forms of local churches that in their essential relationality interact with each other in a dynamic of cross-cultural living.

---

[15] Stanislas Breton, *The Word and the Cross*, trans. Jacquelyn Porter (New York: Fordham University Press, 2002), esp. 1–11. See also Stanislas Breton, *Écriture et Révélation* (Paris: Ed. du Cerf, 1979).

Overcoming Forgetting in Keeping Memory

As we gather for Eucharist, we are pressed to ask how our remembrance of Christ includes those who suffer, those who are almost forgotten within the church's own eucharistic symphony, and those who have passed from this earth and may by forgetfulness be forced out of history. There is much to be learned from Julia Kristeva's distinction between the energies that are incorporated symbolically into the social order and those that are left symbolically marginal, even designed to place people in such a way that they are to find their life's direction at the margins.[16] Others, such as Rosemary Radford Ruether[17] and Sean McDonagh,[18] remind us of the forgetfulness of creation or of our readiness to embrace it only in a symbolic expression of human dominance. Meditation on the Word of God within eucharistic gatherings opens up afresh the possibilities of appropriating the divine justice given through revelation. Even while appealing to Eucharist as foundational, we have to be ready to widen its intake and its horizons. We need to learn to pray from the point of view of the marginal and of cultures and ethnic groups that look for their location in a postcolonial world and in the effort to give voice to all creation in its travail. We even need to give voice to the dead, especially to those who have passed by violence or passed unceremoniously from life.

The Spirit, indwelling love and discernment, inspires the church to make its own the testimony of the word and cross of Jesus Christ, testimony to the name of God as Love. In this very appropriation the Spirit moves us to love of the other, to a practical and discerning love which holds on to nothing for oneself and yields all for the sake of the other. The self and consciousness of self cedes to what is testified in Christ, through and in his members, for whom he has given himself, in death and in sacrament, in love. By force of the indwelling Spirit, those who love in Christ hold no form or representation of the event remembered or of the community formed above the call of love. They hold on to nothing, in the urge to embrace through action, and give vitality and a

---

[16] See, for example, Julia Kristeva, *The Kristeva Reader*, ed. Toril Moi (New York: Columbia University Press, 1986), 34–88.

[17] Among her works, see Rosemary Radford Ruether, *Womanguides: Readings toward a Feminist Theology* (Boston: Beacon Press, 1985), 195–245.

[18] Sean McDonagh, *Passion for the Earth: The Christian Vocation to Promote Justice, Peace and the Integrity of Creation* (Maryknoll, NY: Orbis Books, 1994), 103–46.

place within God's love to others. The self-emptying or *kenosis* of Christ on the cross calls forth the self-emptying of those who are his disciples, a self-emptying which acknowledges the limits of all representation and is ready to cross out whatever representations hinder the gift of love and its testimony in the breadth and universality of God's giving.

The memorial of Christ and the assurance of his gift promise us that he is present through the redeeming and life-giving Spirit in all things human and, indeed, in all that was created good. All people's histories, and today the intermeshing that we name global history, are engaged when we keep eucharistic memorial. Openness to cultures easily becomes folkloric, embellishing the liturgy with sounds, with colour, with sweet-smelling odours. And perhaps even with some colourful language. To go deeply into the presence of Christ, to his narrative and sacramental presence, we have to ask how these people are redeemed in their own history, in their own anamnestic solidarity with their own past.

Today, following John Paul, we speak of the purification of memories, that is, of their confession and redemption.[19] Among other things, he has spoken of the memories of what was suppressed in the work of evangelization by European missionaries on other continents and in the midst of peoples of other cultures. While the gift of the Gospel of Jesus Christ which they brought is not to be forgotten, mixed up with this there are the memories of how the European church compromised itself with the work of colonization and the suppression or marginalization of other cultures. In remembering, we are oddly quite adept at forgetting, and then at forgetting what we have forgotten. No people is able to move away from its past, especially from its tragic past, without keeping its memories alive and without seeking reconciliation with its destiny, without looking for hope through redemption of the past. The hope is expressed in a remembrance that draws poetically on the Scriptures and the Christian tradition, looking for promise in the memory of what God has wrought through Word and Spirit. As one Jewish writer has put it in his own appeal to Jewish tradition, "between time lost and time remembered, lies the work of art."[20]

---

[19] John Paul II, *The Mystery of the Incarnation: Bull of Indiction of the Great Jubilee Year of 2000* (Boston: Pauline Books and Media, 1999).

[20] Cited by David N. Power, "Foundations for Pluralism in Sacramental Expression: Keeping Memory," *Worship* 75 (2001): 194–209.

Such poetic hope, wrought out of remembrance of a tragic past, belongs within the history of suffering and injustice but changes it into a remembrance of history that cannot be emptied of divine promise. Here we are concerned with the remembrance of their past, in all its creativity and tragedy, by peoples who profess Christ, the crucified and risen. In the fullness of the memory of Word and Spirit, we can see that God has been and is at work in all histories, but what can be said of seeing them in the light of Christ, of Christ's willing identification through suffering with those who have suffered? In keeping eucharistic memorial, the church can forget nothing, however harsh. It cannot forget Christ and it cannot forget forgetting the history of those whom it called to the faith in the very work of evangelization and sacrament.

Now the work remains to be done, that of remembering the sufferings of peoples, gathering into eucharistic communion those whose stories have been for too long omitted. It is insufficient to say that in its Eucharist the church is in communion with those who have gone to rest in the peace of Christ. Their memory also has to be gathered into the communion, their deaths redeemed for the sake of peoples and the sake of humanity.

Looking even beyond the Christian fellowship, John Paul II has shown how this is done in addressing the ovens at the extermination camp of Mauthausen, calling on the Jewish people who died there to speak. Those who have passed on have voices. They are survivors in our own survival or tragically perhaps they die once again through their posterity's failures to remember. Tragic memories often have to do with the dead, but they remain alive in those who have inherited them in their flesh, who live by the consequences of past events that caused pain and tragedy. The present stories of those who live in the inheritance of old stories are important to our eucharistic memorial. It may be the migrant family struggling to find a place in an alien country that carries the past in its flesh. It may be those who still carry the wounds of past slavery and injustice but are nourished by the accounts or hymns or devotions of spiritual struggle. It may be the women who still have to rescue their present and future, in both civil and religious society, from the memories of centuries of discrimination but are yet enlivened by the memories of those women who, though placed at the margins of the symbolic order, exercised their varied prophetic and charismatic ministry over the centuries.

Pope Benedict, in turn, drew the connection between Eucharist and the current misfortunes of environmental destruction. He has spoken of "a Eucharistic spirituality capable of changing the fabric of society," a spirituality that he says in his 2009 message for the day of World Peace is antidote to the race for energy which is inspired by the quest for profit and which despoils particular peoples on this earth, preventing them from using their own resources and developing their own ways of life, in the places to which they belong.[21]

As the world becomes more conscious of the ecological crisis that overshadows it because of the ways humanity has exploited and even used up the resources of the earth, the eschatological horizon of eucharistic remembrance has to include a hope for the restoration of the peaceable kingdom, for a more just relationship between humans and other creatures, between humans and the resources of life offered by existence on this planet.

As John Paul II and Benedict XVI remind us, the embrace of Christians is vaster than that of the Christian story: it stretches out arms, like Christ on the cross, to all humanity and to every lost world. Since as Christians we take our place in the community of peoples and affirm that God redeems all, our eucharistic memory must include the memory of Auschwitz, the memory of Rwanda, the memory of apartheid, the memory of slavery, the memory of multiple impoverishment of peoples, and the memory of how in the name of progress people have impoverished earth itself. How the Divine Trinity communicates itself by gift even under such conditions is core to its consideration as a source of human communion, as the energy whereby human communion and communion with the earth comes about and justice is restored.

Eucharistic Redress: Engaging Justice at the Common Table

Like all symbols, the symbols of divine gift have to be imbedded in the lifeworld. When symbol systems clash, the lifeworld is fractured. Some thoughtful distancing from the symbols and from the lifeworld can be helpful in the retrieval of language when perceptions of reality clash. One must then hope "for the poet," for the one who can bring symbolic expression to birth again in an overcoming of conflict, in a new orientation of vigour emerging from the crisis. Eucharistic language in its inbuilt possibilities of creativity is to be the language of a feeling and thinking subject, individuals

[21] Accessed February 20, 2009, at http://www.vatican.va/holy_father/benedict_xvi/messages/peace/documents/hf_ben-xvi_mes_20081208_xlii-world-day-peace_en.html.

who strive for expression and thought, communities that cohere as intersubjective in their rooting in traditions. From within traditions they may look toward new horizons in a rereading of events and root metaphors. Prophets living under the covenant reread the law and Exodus from a situation of loss. The gospels and Paul reread the rereading of prophets from a situation of disengagement from the letter of the law and through engagement with the Spirit of the law as a story of victory becoming a story of suffering, in which God is "even more" engaged as the one who delivers. It is in such rereading that it continues to serve as theological foundation.

Associating the Word of God with the eucharistic table and the invocation of the Spirit needs ever-increasing attention. On the rediscovery of the liturgy of the Word in the vernacular there was considerable enthusiasm. There was also some application to this part of the liturgy of theories of causality, applying an analogous understanding of sacramental efficacy to scriptural proclamation. This went with high demands on homiletics, as though the homily of the priest by itself could unveil the meaning of the Word for life to the faithful.

In considering the power of the Word of God in the lives of Christian communities, it is not possible to restrict this to the actual moments of Sunday celebration, especially where we have to do with liturgies regulated by the clock. With the Sunday celebration there goes the time given to meditation and exchange on the Scriptures incorporated into the life of the congregation over the week or for a protracted period on the Sunday itself. The Synod on the Word of God held in Rome in 2008 recommended a constant community exchange of this sort. Among other things, it pointed to the influence that this has on issues of justice. Proposition 39 of the recommendations voted at the end of the synod noted how the Word of God when appropriated into people's lives "helps minds and hearts to understand and to love all human realities and all of creation." With this it associated reading the signs of the times in the light of the Scriptures, leading to a commitment to struggle with those "who suffer and who are victims of injustice." If the Word is heard in this way, it can be a guide to engagement in political and social life. We know well that such hearing and interpreting needs the work of the Spirit, giving a vision of love and a divine empathy which is a necessary part of true appropriation of God's revelation.

Proposition 54 for its part associated the hearing of the Word with ecological questions. Receiving the Word, it notes, "generates a new way of seeing things, promoting an authentic ecology, which has its deepest roots in the obedience of faith that receives the Word of God." Knowledge of the Scriptures shows us how this is gained especially from reading Wisdom literature on the action of God in the universe and from the parables of Jesus. In light of his citation of the book of Isaiah at the beginning of his mission in Nazareth, it is also seen how in being a prophetic commitment to the people it is also about right relations with the land given to them by covenant.

When it is imbedded in the Scriptures in this way, eucharistic language engages the confrontation with evil, the surd that infects the world in which we live, and the situations in which we intend to do good. There is always the counterposition of good and evil, of life and death, of light and darkness, of suffering and deliverance, and the power of the Just who suffers within the dominion of death to deliver from death. Thus the language of trinitarian movement is located within the world of sin, as the speech of those who are subject to sin and death but look to God. Using the language of liberation, transformation, hope, God is known in the act in which he is addressed, within the world where freedom to do good and freedom to do evil are caught in apocalyptic contest. On the part of the community, there is the effort to "speak oneself," to find the resources within oneself, the insight into oneself that makes thought and action possible. But this breaks down in the face of evil. So speaking has to be in virtue of a word and a movement of Spirit that is divine gift: only in hearing does the church learn to speak; only in receiving does it learn to act—always a *passio* that is ground to *actio*. If the church does not know how to suffer it does not know how to act.

At the eucharistic gathering, around the two tables of word and sacrament, a community may become more conscious of the issues of justice that it needs to address and redress. This happens, however, only if there is some redress of the ways in which Eucharist itself is celebrated in memorial of Christ's Pasch.

When Jewish peoples from the beginning gathered for Pasch or for the Sabbath meal, it was the time to remember the travail through which they had passed and to allow place also for those at any time suffering under human oppression. Indeed, one of the great tasks of the revision of Jewish liturgies in recent times has been to include the Holocaust, to remember the suffering of peoples endured under all pogroms, to ask how in such travail God could be seen and present. As Christian peoples, we have to ask what memories are called forth at the eucharistic table to be incorporated into the memorial of Christ, to be seen as the locus of the power of the eschatological Spirit at work in bringing to being the reconciliation of all things in Christ, in obedience and submission to the Father. When whole peoples are deprived not simply of food and drink and habitation but of their very cultural heritage, the sign of the bread and the cup make the Eucharist the place for the recall of the memories of those in whose realities the Word takes flesh, with whose history, often tragic, he makes himself one in eager longing.

The eucharistic covenant celebrated by disciples of Christ makes them ask how a people's impoverishment, its cultural privation, its hunger, and its landlessness is to be atoned in Christ. There is the place to pursue that evocation and purification of memories which John Paul sought in convoking the Jubilee Year of 2000. This meant memories of past deeds out of harmony with the Gospel, sinful and hurtful to others, but this cannot be done without the memories that remain alive in those who suffered of hurt done, of injury inflicted, and of deprivation endured. In wanting to become itself the pure sacrifice offered to God in obedience to the Gospel, the church has to become a harbour, a haven for all who, facing truth, recall injuries done and injuries received, and who still suffer the burden of affliction, past and present. Only out of pain acknowledged may life be born anew; only from the cauterization of healing may wounds be cleansed and sweetened by the balm of salving oil. The experiment of truth and reconciliation is that of those who dare to gather at the eucharistic table. All such effort flows from and feeds what is recalled and mourned and celebrated around the twofold table of word and sacrament.

Among the apologies sought during the Jubilee of 2000 we find some pointers to what has to be present in eucharistic gathering. When the Gospel and the proclamation of the Gospel were brought by European missionaries to Africa, to the Americas, to Asia, they not only showed disregard for people's religious and cultural traditions and for their histories but frequently denounced them and required a repudiation of what was native if faith in Christ were to be professed. If this apology made and invited from others by John Paul II is to ring true, the memories and cultural perspectives of these peoples need to be more fully present in ecclesial gatherings. Their histories need to be told, reaching into ancient times. What is remembered by them in their very bodies has to be respected, with regard, for example, to healing traditions, to sacramental signs, and to the remembrance of ancestors, in which the signs of the

Spirit are discernible, acts and things akin to the "spiritual sacrifices" of which the author of 1 Peter speaks.[22] In these are represented a people's resources, that life out of which they may now live in Christ.

Memories now have to include those who at this very time continue to suffer the injustices inflicted by globalization and by the exploitation of natural resources. These were their lands; they are inhabited by their ancestors; they are the places in which the heritage of peoples developed and grew. Resolving land disputes, the use of earth's resources, cannot happen without asking who these people are, how their cultural memories are attached to this place, what rights they now have as peoples. Word and the symbols of food and drink may serve to make these memories with their grief and their joy present at table, provided consecration is not used to camouflage what is bitter in the memories.

The churches themselves can show disregard for the peoples and their lands in the materials they use for keeping memorial of the Saviour. If the symbols of food and drink are not taken from the earth on which they live and have lived, from the land and the waters which they have nurtured and from which for ages unknown they have been fed, this is a serious obstacle to including a people's own memories and values in the memorial of Christ. It is time to think of the materials used for Eucharist as an issue of justice and of true commitment to the transformation of people's lives and histories, to see in them God's blessings and God's pleasure.

Apologies were also made to women during the Jubilee of 2000, and, of course, the injuries done and needing to be remembered vary from place to place. The forgiveness necessitated by such memory has to be extended to church and to the patriarchies with which in its own male dominance it had often allied itself, apologies signaling the need for a retrieval of life-giving forces, not certainly as yet completed. If this purification is to ring true, we have to be touched at the very heart of eucharistic celebration, wounded in the flesh of Christ, wounded in the symbolic exchange of our ecclesial claims. The marginalization and inferiorization of women through the encoded symbol system of the memorial of the Lord cannot go any longer unnoticed. If it does, this does not simply hurt women but it keeps a cultural wound open.

Even at this writing we are assailed by another set of memories with which we scarcely know how to cope. This is the memory of the victims

---

[22] See, for example, Buti Tlhagale "The Gospel Seed on African Soil," *Worldwide: The Church in Southern Africa; Open to the World* 16, no. 2 (2006): 13–18.

who suffered abuse at the hands of priests, religious, and other church workers. Since the injury done was so often done by those who claimed to stand at the altar *in persona Christi,* the memory of abuse is almost inevitably present at every Mass and needs to find therein a proper expression rather than being reduced to the complicity of silence.

When memories such as those adumbrated are allowed expression, then it is possible to ask how Christ as God's Word and how the Spirit as divine life, free and energize what is a cultural and historical heritage. There are indeed forces in the past and in the present from which people may be liberated when Christ is celebrated as Saviour and as Healer. When they are weakened by dark powers, by economic and bodily woes (today, for example, the HIV/AIDS epidemic), or by being at the poor end of global economies, peoples try to placate the forces over which they feel they have no control. Placating, however, they succumb. To remember Jesus Christ as one who takes on their flesh and their history, under whatever names seem appropriate, is the promise of an energy born within them when they are reborn of the water and the Spirit. With a good sense of their own historical significance and of what is the positive history of their past, people know the energies which Christ assumes and transforms and makes the channels of God's eschatologically oriented triune life, that life which on this earth brings the promise of the justice of a more just exchange.

True indeed, in face of all injustice we know ourselves justified only by the justice that God imparts. In face of all sin, we know no forgiveness other than that of God, embodied in its various ways in the efforts of true reconciliation and healing. In various messages for the annual Day of Peace at the beginning of the calendar year, John Paul spoke of the common concern of peoples for peace, noting that peace is founded in justice and that justice is not possible without forgiveness.[23] Key words of such messaging are: communion, peace, justice, forgiveness. If in Christian perspective we wish to give others rights to life and to a place in human society, this is grounded not in merit but in an impulse of generosity that is truly divine, even when it is lodged in human hearts.

At bottom, then, there is the question: what liberating and creative forces emerge from keeping memories alive and grafting them into the memorial of Christ, or, from another point of view, grafting the memorial

---

[23] For example, John Paul II, "Message for World Peace Day 2002," *Origins* 31 28 (2001): 461–66.

of Christ unto them? In sacramental and spiritual terms, what power of the Spirit at work in humanity and in creation is revealed in the act of keeping memory? To what is the memorial of Christ's Pasch brought and what is brought from the story of a people to the memorial of Christ?

Conclusion

While exercising a foundational role in ordering the life of the church and giving place to the life of the Trinity within it, eucharistic celebration itself has been influenced by social and cultural ordering that is not biblically rooted. As a *locus theologicus*, therefore, it has to be critically considered, in the awareness that the ordering of celebration and the formulation of prayer creates the milieu and the lifeworld in which it is possible to reflect on the gift of divine life and the gift of divine justice to the world.

The connection with justice is that the life poured out and given expression is spoken eschatologically. It names a justice that belongs to the present time in memory of Christ and in anticipation of the future. It places the present under judgment in light of these two poles and disrupts the "course of events." It employs the speech of narrative foundation, harking to a word spoken, thanking for what is given and what is anticipated, and petitioning for God's justice and for eternal life. The narrative foundation gives the interpretive metaphor of memorial recall and differs across traditions, but it is always suggestive of a justice that is given by God alone and a communion which is the operation of the Spirit, poured into the hearts of the faithful, to live in communion, to speak, and to witness.

Finally, Eucharist provides grounds for a response in a time when humanity is in face of global communication and movement. We see the need for people to keep culture, community, and lifeworld alive, as the condition of their participation in the new shifts. Faith and its cultural expression may give identity, autonomy, life, and the power to act. The churches, however, need to be just in their promotion of Eucharist and so of community, with due respect for the particularity of peoples within the one communion of faith and life. Without this, they cannot speak for justice in the community of faiths, nations, and peoples, now interconnected globally, since to do otherwise would be to fail the very people whom they aspire to serve.

An approach that would lead to the formulation of a social ethic informed by the central Christian symbol of the Trinity steers clear of any attempt to pin down insights about the Trinity in dogmatic formulations or theological constructs, open always to the possibilities of hermeneutical retrievals from Scripture, worship, and practical piety. This is a way of attending, being alert to the divine energies at work throughout the world in manifold and myriad ways, tuning in to the vital forces pulsing through human life, history, the world, the church. We are thus awakened to life and to a love that energizes, carried in a sea's life currents and flow. It is in life and love that we are immersed, and it is by life and love that we are buoyed up rather than being swallowed alive by forces against which we must fight for our lives.

In such an approach, a beginning is found in the liturgy of the church, the foundation for both the life of the Christian people and for theological inquiry. Pursuing this orientation entails allowing ourselves to be carried in the flow of gift given in the economy of salvation. Worship places us before the gift of God who in love emptied himself of glory in order to appear on the scene of human weakness and vulnerability, identifying with human beings in the concrete circumstances of their lives. This is a God who does not fill in for human want, but is present *amid* it, *amid* human longing and want.

A Christian ethic resting on trinitarian foundations is rooted in the divine as life rather than as dominion. A social ethic might be understood as that which gives direction to fuller life and further human flourishing. Such an ethic is not domineering but, rather, finds its fullest expression in solidarity, forgiveness, and reconciliation. When the ethic is rooted in an understanding of Christ as servant and slave, it puts a bold question mark before political and ecclesiastical orders patterned on domination and submission, since the slave/servant who is the Anointed of God is the very presence of God in the face of prevailing political/ecclesiastical order with its hierarchical social arrangement. In God's Word and Spirit we find ourselves summoned to partake of God's own love or *agape*, which is a reconfiguration of the common ideals of justice. If we are able to know anything at all about the Divine Trinity, it is because we are living in this mystery. In the liturgy we are caught up in the ineffable mystery of the Trinity, immersed in the divine life, and it is only within this context that we can speak of an ethic, or social ethic, that springs from the confession of the triune presence of God in human life and history. This effort to treat in systematic fashion the relationship between Trinity and ethics is at one and the same time a doxological theology steeped in and shaped by the worship of the Christian people.

Suggested Readings

Bieler, Andrea, and Luise Schottroff. *The Eucharist: Bodies, Bread, Resurrection.* Minneapolis: Fortress Press, 2007.
The book relates the Eucharist to questions of justice and memory. It draws to a considerable extent on issues raised by feminist theologies.

Bobrinskoy, Boris. *The Mystery of the Trinity: Trinitarian Experience and Vision in Biblical and Patristic Tradition*, 145–96. Crestwood, NY: St Vladimir's Seminary Press, 1999.
This is a good overview of the relation in the early church between Eucharist, church, Trinity, and eschatological hope.

Chauvet, Louis-Marie. *The Sacraments: The Word of God at the Mercy of the Body*, 117–69. Collegeville, MN: Liturgical Press, 1995.
This is a shortened and simplified version of Chauvet's larger work. In the pages noted the author treats of the Body and the Eucharist.

Power, David N. "Worship and Ecology." *Worship* 84 (2010): 290–308.
———. "Eucharistic Justice." *Theological Studies* 67 (2006): 856–79.
———. "Foundations for Pluralism in Sacramental Expression: Keeping Memory." *Worship* 75 (2001): 194–209.
In these three articles Power looks at the Eucharist in the light of current issues of justice in the world and at the place of memory in incorporating this into eucharistic celebration.

Four Currents

We wrote earlier in this volume of the four pillars on which, according to the *Catechism of the Catholic Church*, the Christian life is founded and which are in all things interconnected. In fact, we have thought of them less as pillars and more as currents of life that converge and bring the church into the mystery of divine communion.

Since we made a praxis option, concerned with the flow of life which generates ethical behaviour, the service of justice, and peace in the whole human family, we have related the other currents to the moral life, to an ethic. Communities or lone prophets are prompted by the Spirit, drawn by the Father, to hear and act according to the revealed Word which has its fullness in the incarnation, ministry, death, and resurrection of Jesus of Nazareth. We thought of how, in virtuous action in the service of justice, the life of the Trinity may be discerned in those movements of Word and Spirit which appear in the world as gifts of the Father and lead people to their destiny, so that they come to share forever in the life of this movement of the Three. This is what ennobles the Christian community. This is that Christian dignity to which faith draws attention. Seeking justice is the way of love, the fulfilment in every place and in all places, in every time and in all times, of the basic precept of the love of God and neighbour.

As we consider this praxis view of the divine mystery, we are constantly called to read and reread the Torah and the Beatitudes of the gospel. These point us to the kind of community which is a prophetic presence and to the key components of what is called a virtue ethic (*actio*) which springs from the heart of suffering (*passio*). Such an ethic is grounded in what is discerned as good and true as it comes from Word and Spirit. Living this ethic is rooted in and grows through an awareness of the beauty springing from the breast pierced by pain.

132

Living as brothers and sisters, seeking the communion of all in the draw toward a common destiny, the church gathers as the Body of Christ in liturgical communion, the climax of which is participation at the communion table of the Lord's Body and Blood. This is an action of hearing, praying, and bonding, leading ever to contemplation of the mystery represented. To grasp the fullness of this mystery, to find it as the heart of the Christian service of justice, we have to feel it and experience it as concretely as Irenaeus describes it (*Against Heresies* 5.2). He first draws attention to the fact that those who gather through the bread and wine, which they confect from the fruits of the earth, are one in and with creation. Without the acknowledgment of their communion in creation, they can neither come to the table nor glimpse the depths of the mystery of Christ. By the Word and Spirit, the two hands of the Father, this bread and wine are transformed into the Body and Blood of Christ, into his flesh given for the life of the world. The Body and Blood of Jesus, his earthly form, are themselves taken from the earth and taken from the human family. It is by this form that Jesus himself, in the living of his mystery, is one with humanity and one with creation. At the communion table, his followers become one with him and in him. Their communion with one another and with the earth is sanctified and perfected. They are his body which continues to live among creatures, his sinews and his lifeblood, the sacramental living form in which he now appears on earth in the power of the Spirit and by which he draws all things to himself, submitting them in obedience to the Father.

The eucharistic gathering is also the place for doing justice, a place where, in making memory of Christ, memory is kept of the living and the dead, of peoples and places, and in a particular way of those who were and are victims, of the suffering of the present time and of the past. It is the place of destiny, of hope of the fulfilment of justice and peace, of that final communion where all share the blessedness of life. It is not only a hope for the future as we saw, for example, in John Paul II's *Ecclesia de Eucharistia* but a firm hope for the present born of a firm commitment in Jesus Christ to the people and the things of earth.

Other kinds of prayer, personal and common, are necessary conjunctives to this eucharistic mystery. Diverse forms of spirituality and of popular piety have nourished communion in the mystery of Christ down through the centuries. In the quest for liberation, more attention has recently been given to how some forms of piety are integral to this struggle and this hope. Jesus Christ is versatile enough to take on different appearances and forms so as to be always with the vast range of his beloved and to let communion with him be nourished and guided by communion with his mother, his disciples, and the saints. In very recent years, an accent has been placed on personal and communal meditation of the Scriptures, on what is called *lectio divina*. This does not replace other kinds of devotion. What it does to engage a faithful people has captured the attention not just of monks but of the poor who find light and hope in the Word.

Doctrine is grounded in the three currents of which we have spoken and is formulated as a guide to people immersed in the mystery. The doctrine of the Trinity is first and foremost about the triune presence and action of God in the world. Even its more abstract formulations, as at Nicea or in Scholastic theology, were intended as guidelines for Christian living, for the life and mission of the church, so that believers might know and believe that the economy of creation and redemption is indeed a divine self-communication, a gift of life that abounds in the world and that has people run toward its fullness in an eternal communion, where God is all in all.

Early preoccupations with right doctrine, for example, those of Athanasius, defender of the faith and formulator of the Creed of Nicea, who in his zeal could by turns be bitter and cruel, kind and loving, show how much preoccupation with divinity is sparked by the conviction about God's gift and presence:

> He is God, the living and creative God of the universe, the Word of the good God, who is God in his own right. The Word is different from all created things: he is the unique Word belonging only to the good Father. This is the Word that created this whole world and enlightens it by his loving wisdom. He who is the good Word of the good Father produced the order in all creation, joining opposites together and forming from them one harmonious sound. He is God, one and only-begotten, who proceeds in goodness from the Father as from the fountain of goodness and gives order, direction, and unity to creation. By his eternal Word the Father created all things and implanted a nature in his creatures. He did not want to see them tossed about at the mercy of their own natures and so be reduced to nothingness. But in his goodness he governs and sustains the whole of nature by his Word (who is himself also God), so that under the guidance, providence, and ordering of that Word, the whole of nature might remain stable and coherent in his light.[1]

[1] Athanasius, *Discourse against the Arians*, nn. 40–42, PG 25, 29–83.

Respecting the efforts of others to speak of the inner Trinity as a communion of persons, or to explain how suffering itself belongs to the life of the Trinity in its free gift of divine life, we have nonetheless eschewed this task. It is the fundamental persuasion of this work that access to the glory of divine communion is had by living within the economy of God's revelation, the economy of the work of Word and Spirit in the world. We know and affirm that the consummation of the divine justice by which we are justified and by which we seek justice on earth is to be consummated in an eternal communion. As Eucharistic Prayer III of the Roman Rite puts it, to live eternally is to be satiated by the glory of God, to be there where all tears are wiped away, where people are like unto the God whom they see, and to live most pleasantly in praising the glory of the Father, through the Son and in the Spirit. Ascending to God through the Word and the Spirit whom he has given us, we do indeed know of the being of God by letting this Word and Spirit work within us and among or between us. It is indeed truly God who is there in Word and Spirit, in a Word vaster than the words through which Word speaks and in a Love more tremendous than our loving in this Love. This speaks to us of what it is in God that pours out in this way. If orthodoxy has stressed both the distinction and the *perichoresis* of Father, Word/Son, and Spirit, it is to speak of a reality in God which we barely glimpse but which is described for us as divine engagement in Word and Love. These are so connected that the Love ever outstrips the Word and the Word outstrips the Love. Yet they are in a constant dance that shows God forth in his own ineffable being. Living, then, by Word and Spirit we ascend into God, partake of this life, hope to dwell in that world of ineffable speech and ineffable love where there is distinction without separation.

What a marvel it would be to live in a world where word speaks only truth and truth shines in reality, where love never betrays the truth and what is spoken never betrays the love. Through these Three—the Father who sends forth, the Word who is sent, and the Spirit who descends—we may truly commune with the being of God. But while these Three are in God and the two come forth from God breathing the cry Abba, we heed the warning of Gregory of Nyssa: in the eternal life of God, while there are Three, it would be foolish for us to count three one by one, to add them up. Keeping "a sustained interest in what may be said of God *in esse*, as well as in what may be known of God through reason illumined by faith, there is an abiding recognition that whatever claims are made about God, or the divine attributes, or God's intention for the world, they are at best partial and incomplete and our grasp on grace quite tenuous."[2] But rather than shunning or setting aside considerations about God's being in three or about our being in God triune, we simply enter "the doxology of the heart, the culmination of prayer beyond words and thoughts, though fostered by both."[3] Word and Love allow us to see the "diamond absolutes"[4] in life as we live it, in realities as we encounter Christ in them. And so we know the world may hope and live out its being in that hope arising from the present moment transformed.

> May your love be upon us, O Lord, as we place all our hope in you.
>
> (Psalm 33:22)

> For there is hope of a tree, if it be cut down, that the tender branch thereof will not cease.
>
> (Job 14:7; KJV)

[2] Michael Downey, "*Lex Orandi, Lex Credendi*: Taking it Seriously in Systematic Theology," in *A Promise of Presence*, ed. Michael Downey and Richard N. Fragomeni (Washington, DC: OCP, 1992), 3–25, at 16.

[3] Ibid.

[4] Seamus Heaney, "Exposure," in *North* (New York: Oxford University Press, 1976), 73.

Index